Quick & Easy

Pillows & Cushions

Quick & Easy
Pillows &
Cushions

50 STEP-BY-STEP PROJECTS

CICO BOOKS
LONDON NEW YORK

Published in 2010 by CICO Books
an imprint of Ryland Peters & Small
519 Broadway, 5th Floor, New York NY 10012
20–21 Jockey's Fields, London WC1R 4BW

www.cicobooks.com

10 9 8 7 6 5 4 3 2 1

A CIP catalog record for this book is available from the Library
of Congress and the British Library.

ISBN-13: 978 1 907030 63 5

Printed in China

Compiled by Gail Abbott
Editor: Alison Wormleighton
Design: Roger Hammond, BlueGum
Photography: see page 176
Illustration: see page 176

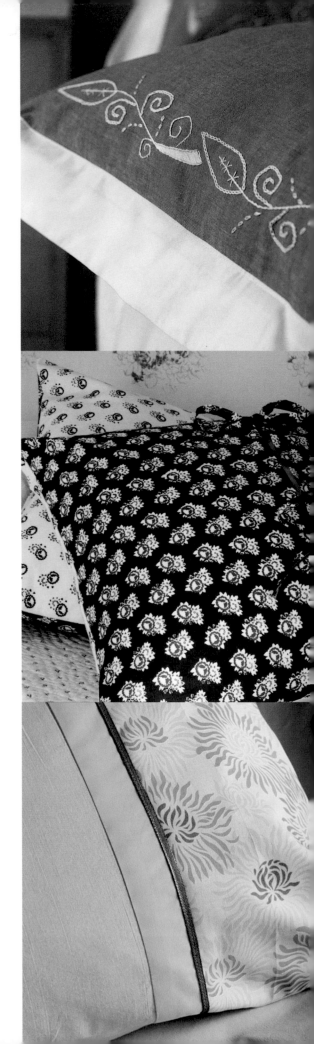

contents

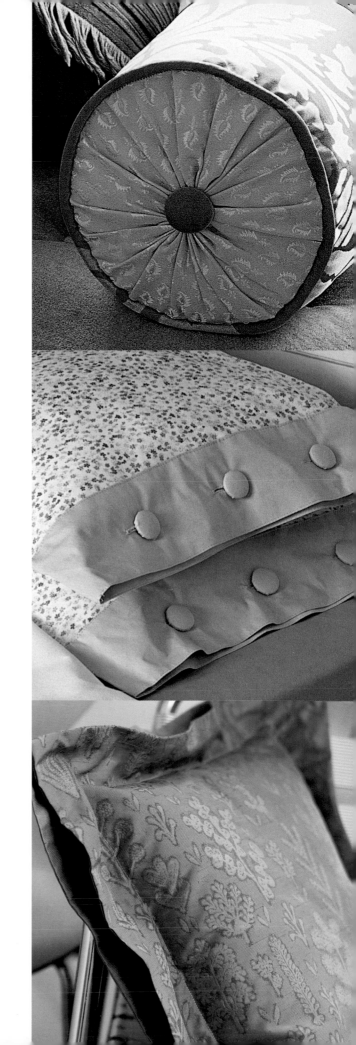

introduction

There's no doubt about it, whether you are starting from scratch with a newly decorated room that needs color and pattern or whether you want to give a tired, down-at-heel sofa a new lease on life, a new set of cushions or pillows will be one of the easiest—and most budget-conscious—ways to set about it. Cushions and pillows plump up a sofa or armchair and always make a relaxing place to rest and loll; a bed piled with pillows looks inviting and welcoming, and the clever use of cushions will introduce a bright patch of color, or bring harmony to a mismatched scheme. Hard surfaces can be transformed with cushions, too. An unforgiving wooden bench in the garden becomes a place to sit and read, or simply to drink a cup of tea and take some time out. An aluminum garden seat, brought indoors, is transformed into a comfortable dining chair with the addition of a quilted seat pad. A set of old wooden kitchen chairs, lifted with a dash of paint and a ruffled cushion, can turn a dull kitchen into a retreat for the family to gather at mealtimes. Pillows and cushions have the ability to transform a bench, a chair, a bed, or a whole room.

Something for everyone

Making your own pillows and cushions might mean learning a whole new set of skills—and for beginners every project in this book has a set of easy step-by-step illustrations to guide you through the process. The simplest pillows have a tie fastening or just a button or two to close, and you can progress onto learning how to put in a zipper when you have conquered the basics. Make one of the easiest projects and slowly progress by adding a few extras, like a bit of fancy embellishment. Or see if you can tackle a simple patchwork project that uses a few different fabrics. You might want to pick up a skill you learned years ago and give yourself a challenge—and for those with advanced skills there are plenty of projects that will take time and experience, like the Log Cabin Pillow or Crazy Velvet Patchwork. Sewing a pillow is usually no more than an evening's work, but it's a great way to make an immediate difference to your home, or to create a gift for a friend or an heirloom to hand down.

Above: Traditional log cabin patchwork is given an attractive modern twist (see pages 80–83 for instructions).

Opposite: Flirty frills transform a garden chair (see pages 158–160 for instructions).

It's best to approach the way you use pillows with creativity and spontaneity, but there are a few simple guidelines that will help. Too many different colors and patterns used together can look overwhelming, but an over-coordinated set can look self-conscious and a little stiff. Mixing together different patterns works best if you stick to a two-color scheme—blue and white, or terra-cotta and cream, for example. You can combine stripes, checks, florals, and polkadots all piled together if they share the same basic color theme. If your idea is to use a varied range of colors, proceed more cautiously and pick fabrics with a limited range of patterns. A riotous set of colorful pillow fabrics will work well used together if they are united in sharing a floral, geometric, or striped design.

Above: A classically elegant embroidered linen pillow (see pages 116–118 for instructions).

Sophisticated effects

Although color is fashionable again, many of us still love to decorate our rooms in pale, neutral shades, and this is a perfect solution if you are less than confident with color. The key to making this type of scheme work is to be flamboyant with texture. The feel of crunchy linen, the luxury of soft velvet, the raised touch of a hand-embroidered monogram, or the added texture of a fringed braid… all these can be put together if the basic colors are white, cream, or neutrals. Vintage linen and flour sacks are available at fairs and on websites, and these can be turned into pillows with texture and patina that will make all the difference to a monochrome scheme. Without changes in texture, you are in danger of living in a bland, featureless room that has no focal point, so a pile of pillows on the sofa or bed is the perfect solution.

Making your own cushions or pillows means you can make the most of bargains if you look for remnants of fabrics that would otherwise be out of your price bracket. A room can be decorated for very little if you use a basic white paint for the walls and woodwork, or turn one of the walls into a feature with a block of color, but you can lift it onto a whole new plane if you make a pillow or two with a designer fabric on sale at a reduced price. Use the expensive fabric for the fronts only, and make the backs from a cheaper material. Scouring secondhand stores or

flea markets might mean you unearth a pair of faded but still beautiful velvet curtains that can be cut up to make pillows; or use your imagination and patch areas of an embroidered tablecloth together, recycle a vintage dress, or give a new lease on life to a wool blanket. Have fun, and remember that you can be as flamboyant and original as you like when it comes to making pillows and cushions. They are the perfect small project for learning to sew, for helping you decorate your first home, or for getting down to some ingenious creativity.

Above: Fun yo-yo patchwork circles make a pretty and feminine pillow cover (see pages 132–133 for instructions).

Simple
pillows

Making your own pillows can be a satisfying way to learn to sew even if you are a complete beginner. If you can sew a straight seam most of these easy projects will be within your reach, and they are all closed without the need to insert a zipper. Making a simple pillow will take only an evening and is the perfect way to transform your living space with color and pattern.

striped and piped pillow

This striped pillow is a classic design that would be equally at home in a colonial-style room or a pared-down minimalist interior. The striped front contrasts well with the plain linen back, while the brightly colored piping, carefully chosen to coordinate with the stripes, gives definition to the square shape. Self-covered buttons on the back of the cover provide the perfect finishing touch.

You will need

+ striped fabric for front
+ plain fabric for back
+ solid-colored fabric for piping
+ 80 in. (2m) of thick piping cord
+ two 2½ x 20 in. (6 x 50cm) strips of lightweight fusible interfacing
+ dressmaker's fading pen or tailor's chalk
+ five 1 in. (2.5cm) self-cover buttons
+ 20 in. (50cm) square pillow
+ matching sewing thread

1 From striped fabric, cut out one 21¼ in. (53cm) square. From plain fabric, cut out one 21¼ in. (53cm) square and one 8 x 21¼ in. (20 x 53cm) strip. From the solid-colored fabric, cut out one 2½ x 80 in. (6 x 200cm) bias strip (see page 169). Baste the bias strip over the piping cord with wrong sides together. Baste it in place on the right side of the front panel, allowing for a ⅝ in. (1.5cm) seam, and join the ends as shown on page 169. Press under a narrow hem along one side of the square back panel, then press under 2½ in. (6cm) and unfold.

2 Following the manufacturer's directions, iron a strip of interfacing along the inside of the second fold. Press the hem under again to cover the interfacing. Baste it down just inside the fold. Reinforce one long edge of the back strip in the same way.

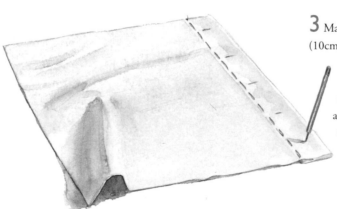

3 Mark the position of five buttonholes at 4 in. (10cm) intervals on the right side of the back panel using a dressmaker's fading pen or tailor's chalk. The first buttonhole should lie 2 in. (5cm) from the raw edge and start ¾ in. (2cm) from the fold. Sew the buttonholes by hand or by machine.

4 With right sides together and raw edges even, place the back panel over the piped front panel. Pin in place. Pin the back strip along the remaining edge, right side down, then baste all three pieces together.

5 Fit a zipper foot or piping foot to the sewing machine, then stitch all around the edge, close to the piping cord. Trim the corners and turn right side out. Press lightly. Cover the buttons with striped fabric, following the manufacturer's directions. Mark their positions on the back strip and sew them in place. Insert the pillow and fasten the buttons.

TIP

When using striped fabric for covering buttons, make sure that you select a narrow stripe and center the stripe across the middle of the button.

Cotton ticking is based on fabrics originally used for making mattresses, so is generally tough and hard-wearing. It is available in a wide range of colors and stripe patterns, which work happily together in different combinations. Instead of using a plain fabric for the piping/cording, why not use a strip of the same fabric for a multicolor cord? An alternative to covering the buttons is to use wooden or horn buttons instead.

tied pillow cover

Tied into perky bows, the narrow ties make this pillow cover look pretty and feminine. Using reverse colorways of the same pattern for the front and back of a pillow cover always looks very effective, particularly when you use them in a group of pillows. And if you wish to make the project even simpler, you could use ribbon in a coordinating color for the two sets of ties, rather than making them from matching fabric.

You will need

+ two pieces of fabric measuring the length by two-thirds of the width of your pillow, plus ⅝ in. (1.5cm) all around for seams

+ one piece of contrasting fabric the same size as your pillow, plus ⅝ in. (1.5cm) all around for seams

+ four strips of fabric, each 14 × 1½ in. (35.5 × 4cm)

+ square pillow

+ matching sewing thread

1 For the front, press under ⅝ in. (1.5cm) down one long side of both narrower fabric pieces. Machine stitch the hems in place.

2 Press under another 1½ in. (4cm) down each hemmed edge and press in place to form facings. Baste the raw facing ends in place.

3 Topstitch down one facing edge close to the outer edge. Trim this front piece down to measure half the width of your pillow, plus ⅝ in. (1.5cm) for a seam allowance. Do not trim the other front piece.

4 Lay the contrasting piece right side up on a flat surface and place the narrow front right side down on it, with the raw edges even. Place the wider front on top, right side down, overlapping the hemmed edges and keeping raw edges even. Sew the pieces together around all sides, taking a ⅝ in. (1.5cm) seam.

5 Trim the corners close to the stitching to reduce the bulk. Turn the cover right side out and press.

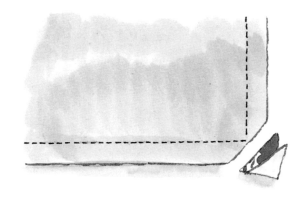

6 With wrong sides together, press one tie strip in half along its length. Open the strip out flat and press the long raw edges over to the wrong side to meet at the central press-line. Also press under ¼ in. (5mm) at each end. Refold the strip with the raw edges inside and machine stitch along the pressed edges through all four layers. Repeat for the remaining tie strips.

7 Lay the cover out flat and use pins to mark the edge of the overlap on the piece of fabric forming the underlap. Using more pins, mark the position of the ties on the front overlap to correspond to the pin line below, placing them roughly a quarter of the way in from the top and bottom edges of the cover.

8 Hand sew the ties to the hem of the front overlap (without sewing through the outer layer of the front) and to the right side of the underlap to correspond. Insert the pillow through the opening and tie the bows to close the cover.

VARIATION

Make a pillow look more romantic by using a pair of wide ribbons in place of the narrower ties you make yourself. Choose a color that coordinates with the pillow cover fabric, or pick a contrasting shade. You can vary the look by the width of ribbon you use. A very narrow ribbon would make three, or even four, sets of ties across the front.

buttoned pillow cover

This elegant pillow cover provides a great way to use monogrammed linen. If you can find monogrammed linen featuring friends' initials, but which is worn out or stained elsewhere on the linen, you can use the monogrammed portion to create a beautiful personalized gift. Large linen napkins with monogrammed initials could also be used for a small pillow, and the fact that napkins would already be hemmed would make the project even quicker.

You will need

+ vintage monogrammed linen sheet, or linen or damask tablecloth or napkins

+ rectangular pillow

+ matching sewing thread

+ two ⅝ in. (1.5cm) buttons

+ dressmaker's fading pen or tailor's chalk

1 With the monogram in the center, cut out a front cover to the dimensions of your pillow, adding a ⅝ in. (1.5cm) seam allowance all around. Cut out one back cover to the same size as the front and a smaller back piece the width of the pillow, by 8½ in. (21.5cm), plus a ⅝ in. (1.5cm) seam allowance all around.

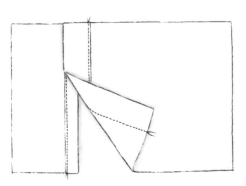

2 On one long edge of the narrow back piece, turn over a ⅝ in. (1.5cm) hem to the right side and press in place. Fold over a further 1½ in. (4cm) hem, press, and machine stitch in place. Repeat on one short edge of the wider back piece, turning over and pressing 1½ in. (4cm) and then a further 2¼ in. (6cm). Stitch the hem in place.

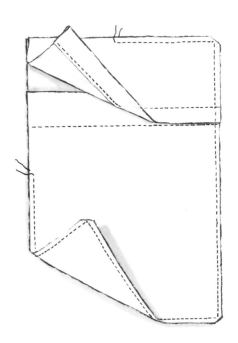

3 Place the front cover and the wider back piece with right sides together and raw edges even. Lay the narrow back piece on top, right side down, overlapping the hemmed edges and keeping raw edges even. Pin and stitch the pieces together around all four edges, taking a ⅝ in. (1.5cm) seam. Trim the corners close to the stitching. Turn the cover right side out and press.

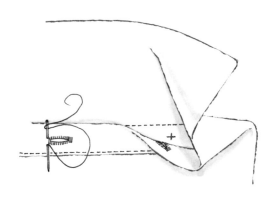

4 Using a fading pen or tailor's chalk, lightly mark the position of two vertical buttonholes centrally along the hem of the overlap on the back opening, spacing them evenly. Make buttonholes by hand or machine. Mark the position of the buttons, through the buttonholes, on the underlap of the back opening, and sew the buttons place. Insert the pillow and fasten the buttons.

It's still possible to find vintage French sheets with hand-embroidered monograms, and although they can be expensive these days, it's not always easy to know where to use them. Use the monogram to grace the center of a pillow made from the same linen for an heirloom pillow to give as a special wedding gift. Make the front of the cover from panels, placing the monogram in the center panel.

loose linen cover

Two squares of cool striped linen with pairs of ties on each side sandwich an inner pillow of contrasting striped fabric. A simple-to-make cover that will make a big impact, this is excellent for giving a quick facelift to older pillows that are looking a little tired.

You will need

+ ¾ yd. (60cm) of striped linen fabric, 45 in. (115cm) wide

+ ⅝ yd. (50cm) of striped cotton fabric, 45 in. (115cm) wide

+ 5½ yd. (5m) of brown cotton tape, 1 in. (2.5cm) wide

+ 5½ yd. (5m) of cream cotton tape, ½ in. (1cm) wide

+ 18 in. (45cm) square pillow

+ matching sewing thread

1 For the outer cover, cut out two pieces of fabric from the striped linen, each 22 in. (55cm) square. Make sure the stripes run parallel with two of the sides. On one piece press under ¼ in. (5mm) all around, then a further ¾ in. (2cm), making sure the stripes match up on the wrong side of the fabric. Repeat for the other piece.

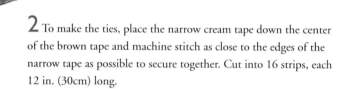

2 To make the ties, place the narrow cream tape down the center of the brown tape and machine stitch as close to the edges of the narrow tape as possible to secure together. Cut into 16 strips, each 12 in. (30cm) long.

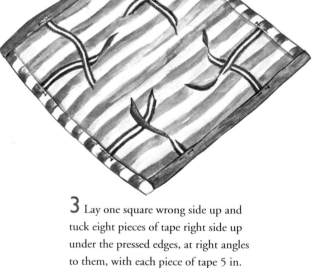

3 Lay one square wrong side up and tuck eight pieces of tape right side up under the pressed edges, at right angles to them, with each piece of tape 5 in. (13cm) from a corner. Pin them in place.

4 To secure the ties to the cover, machine stitch as close as possible to the inner edge of the hems, sewing across each of the ties. Make sure that the ties are straight.

Natural fabrics like these vintage flour sacks add interesting texture to an all-white room. Vintage linens are often hand-woven, so the surface has an integral slubbed effect. Make a couple of simple pillows by stitching around three edges, turning them right side out, and tying them at the remaining edge with tapes.

5 Fold each tie over the seam and press. Machine a second line of stitching ¼ in. (5mm) in from the inner edge to secure the ties facing outward. Press. Attach the ties to the other square in the same way. Slip stitch each open corner closed and trim the raw ends of the ties on the diagonal.

6 To make the inner cover, cut out two pieces from the striped cotton, each 19 in. (48cm) square. With the squares right sides together, pin and machine stitch a ½ in. (1cm) seam on three sides. Turn the cover right side out and press. Insert the pillow and slip stitch the opening. Place in the center of one outer panel (with the panel wrong side up), then put the other panel over it (right side up) and fasten the pairs of corresponding ties.

tailored cover

Give an old pillow a new lease on life by covering it with vintage fabric. This ticking pillow uses antique mother-of-pearl buttons found in a thrift store but, if sewing is not your strong point or you prefer a less tailored look, you could simply stitch together two squares of fabric and attach ribbon or fabric ties.

You will need

+ one piece of fabric the same size as your pillow, plus 1¼ in. (3cm) all around

+ two pieces of fabric the same width as your pillow, plus 1¼ in. (3cm), and half the length of your pillow, plus 4 in. (10cm)

+ three or four buttons or four 9 in. (23cm) lengths of 1 in. (2.5cm) ribbon to tie

+ dressmaker's fading pen or tailor's chalk

+ matching sewing thread

+ pillow

1 Press under ⅜ in. (1cm) and then 2 in. (5cm) on one long edge of each of the two smaller pieces of fabric. Stitch each hem in place.

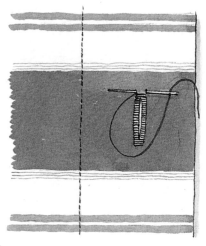

2 Mark the positions of the buttonholes with fading pen or tailor's chalk on the wrong side of one of the smaller piece of fabric about 1 in. (2.5cm) from the hemmed edge. Make the buttonholes by hand or machine.

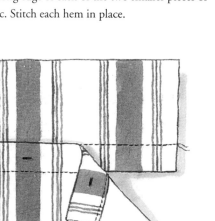

3 Lay the other small piece of fabric right side up on your work surface, and place the piece with the buttonholes on top of it, also right side up, with the hemmed edges in the center and overlapping by about 2 in. (5cm). Check that the overall size is the same as the largest piece, and adjust the overlap if necessary. Baste across the hemmed portion at the side edges.

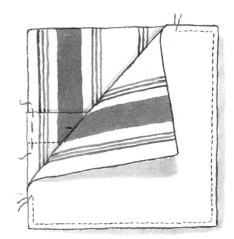

4 Place the largest piece of fabric on top of the other two, right sides together. Machine stitch a ⅝ in. (1.5cm) seam around all four outer edges. Trim the corners. Turn the cover right side out. Insert a pin through the center of each buttonhole into the fabric underneath; sew on a button at each of these points. Insert the pillow in the cover and fasten the buttons.

For a country-style
living room, a mix
of florals and stripes
is always a winner,
because they
complement each
other perfectly.
A basic color scheme
of white and blue
with a dash of red will
look fresh and pretty.

VARIATION

Buttoned pillows make a virtue of
practical fastenings. Turned to the
back, the buttons are functional and
allow the cover to be removed for
washing, but if turned to the front
they become the main feature of
the design. Find a set of decorative
buttons and then ring the changes in
the shape of the pillow. A couple of
rectangular pillows can replace three
or four scatter pillows, and two long
pillows are ample enough to sit
snugly along the back of a sofa, as
pictured here.

floor pillow

Make a pile of comfy floor pillows to sink into with a good book or to provide extra seating when guests come to visit. Use two different fabrics for each pillow and cover the button at the center of each with a coordinating fabric for extra interest. The cover cannot be taken off without removing the buttons, so make sure you use a pillow that is machine washable so that you can throw the whole thing into the machine for easy cleaning.

You will need

+ 26¾ in. (68cm) square of each of two coordinating fabrics

+ 25½ in. (65cm) square pillow

+ two 1¼ in. (3cm) self-cover buttons

+ matching sewing thread

+ upholstery thread and needle

I Lay one fabric square right side up on your work surface and place the second one right side down on top of it, aligning all edges. Pin and machine stitch a ⅝ in. (1.5cm) seam all around, leaving a gap of about 12 in. (30cm) in one side. Trim the corners close to the stitching to reduce the bulk.

2 Turn the cover right side out and press. Insert the pillow and hand sew the opening closed, using small stitches. Find the center point of the cover on both the front and the back and mark with pins.

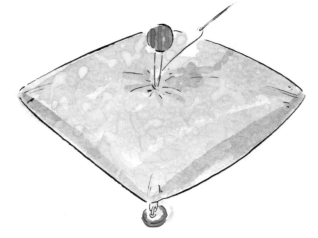

3 Following the manufacturer's directions, cover the buttons with fabric. Thread an upholstery needle with upholstery thread and knot the thread. Sew through the pillow at the central pin and thread on a button. Take the needle back though the pillow and thread a button onto the other side. Pull the thread firmly to pull the buttons into the pillow. Sew back through the buttons several times more, and secure the thread with a few stitches.

VARIATION

For more relaxed and casual floor pillows, make the covers themselves in exactly the same way as shown in the step-by-step directions but omit the central button. Your choice of fabrics will dictate the overall effect, so choose muted colors for a sophisticated scheme and brighter cottons for a child's room. Thrown onto a bare wooden floor, they will make a popular spot for children to relax and play.

floral pillow cover with ties

Add a pretty, country feel to your sofa with these lovely floral pillows. The same fabric has been used throughout, but you could choose a coordinating fabric for the back, so that you can turn the pillow over and change the look to suit your mood. The covers are very easy to make, as they have no zippers or buttons but are fastened with neat little fabric ties. To make them even simpler, you could replace the ties with ribbon.

You will need

+ ¾ yd. (70cm) of floral fabric at least 39 in. (1m) wide

+ matching sewing thread

+ 18 in. (45cm) square pillow

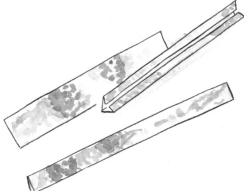

1 Cut a piece of fabric measuring 19 x 19¼ in. (48 x 49cm). Along one short edge, fold over ¼ in. (1cm) and then another ½ in. (1.5cm) to the wrong side. Machine stitch in place.

2 Cut four 3 x 10 in. (7 x 25cm) strips of fabric. Fold each one in half lengthwise, wrong sides together, and press. Open out. Along both long edges, turn in ½ in. (1.5cm) and press. At one short end, turn in ½ in. (1.5cm) and press.

3 Fold the whole strip in half along the center fold line. Machine stitch along the strip, stitching as close to the edge as possible, and across the folded end. Press.

TIP

If you make a pillow cover in a fabric that tends to fray, use a zigzag machine stitch around the pieces before stitching them together.

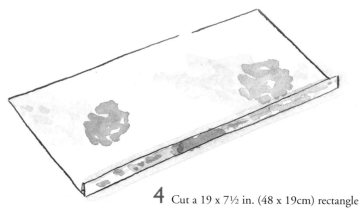

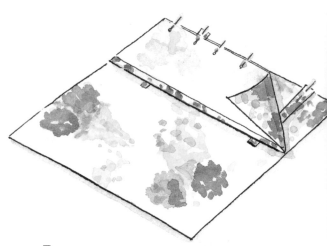

4 Cut a 19 x 7½ in. (48 x 19cm) rectangle of fabric. Along one long edge, fold over ⅜ in. (1cm) and then another ½ in. (1.5cm) to the wrong side. Pin and machine stitch.

5 Cut a 19 in. (48cm) square of fabric. With right sides together, pin the long raw edge of the rectangle to one side of this square. With raw edges even, insert two ties into the seam 4½ in. (12cm) from each corner. Machine stitch a ½ in. (1.5cm) seam. Press the seam open.

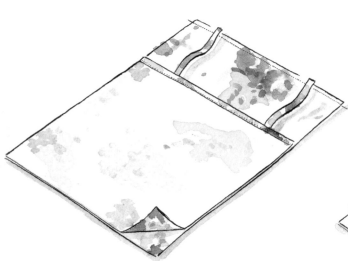

6 Lay this piece right side down on your work surface. With right sides together, place the other fabric piece on top, aligning the hemmed edge with the seam on the bottom piece.

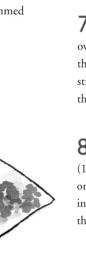

7 Fold the flap over the top and pin and machine stitch around the three sides of the square with a ½ in. (1.5cm) seam, stitching through the folded-over flap as well. Trim the corners. Turn the cover right side out.

8 Take the remaining two ties, fold under ½ in. (1.5cm) at the raw ends and machine stitch them onto the cover, aligning them with the ties already in place. Press the cover. Insert the pillow and tie the pairs of ties in neat bows to close.

If you are a complete novice at sewing, there can't be an easier pillow to make than this one, and omitting the ties makes it even easier. The only skill you will need is to be able to sew a straight seam, so this is a wonderful way to practice your newfound skills. Make them in a variety of florals or solid-color fabrics.

tie-on pillow cover

The informal covers on these giant floor pillows needed a simple approach: They had to be washable and hard-wearing, yet decorative. The slipcovers on the large square pillows are fastened with narrow ties made from the main cover fabric—an unfussy closure that can be undone easily when desired.

You will need

+ main fabric
+ 25 in. (63cm) square pillow with plain cover
+ matching sewing thread
+ knitting needle or blunt pencil

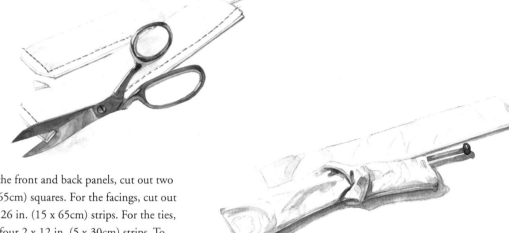

1 For the front and back panels, cut out two 26 in. (65cm) squares. For the facings, cut out two 6 x 26 in. (15 x 65cm) strips. For the ties, cut out four 2 x 12 in. (5 x 30cm) strips. To make the four ties, fold each strip of fabric in half lengthwise, with right sides together. Pin and machine stitch a ½ in. (1cm) seam along the long edge and one short edge. Clip the corners.

2 Turn each tie right side out. Ease the corners into shape using a knitting needle and press the ties flat.

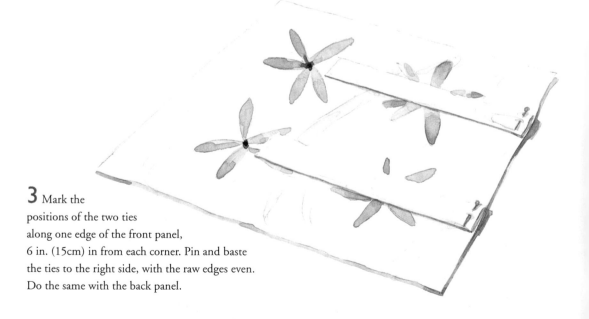

3 Mark the positions of the two ties along one edge of the front panel, 6 in. (15cm) in from each corner. Pin and baste the ties to the right side, with the raw edges even. Do the same with the back panel.

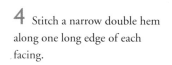

4 Stitch a narrow double hem along one long edge of each facing.

5 With right sides together and raw edges even, pin and baste one of the facings to the front panel. Machine stitch, working an extra row to secure the ends of the ties. Sew the other facing to the back panel in the same way. Press the seams to one side and zigzag all the raw edges.

TIP

Making ties by folding in the raw edges, then folding the strips in half lengthwise and stitching them right side out means that you don't have to struggle with turning the ties right side out at the end.

6 Open out the facings. With right sides together, pin and machine stitch the front and back together, and the facings together, around the three zigzagged edges, taking a ½ in. (1cm) seam.

7 Trim the corners close to the stitching, then press the side seams open. Turn the cover right side out and press the facings to the inside. Machine stitch around the opening, ⅛ in. (3mm) from the edge. Insert the pillow and fasten the ties.

To make an elegant pillow for a sophisticated living room or bedroom, fasten the edges of a cream linen pillow cover with a pair of store-bought tassels instead of handmade ties. The linen edges of this version have been hemmed and embellished with a little drawn-thread work, but simple hemmed edges would look effective, too.

pillowcase with buttons

When you make your own pillowcases, you are not limited to using the extra-wide fabrics normally used to make bed linen—you can choose from a larger selection of cotton dress fabrics. This standard pillowcase is made from a delicate cotton fabric with tiny sprigs of flowers. It has a border in a solid color that complements the flower pattern and is finished with three buttons covered in the same cotton fabric.

You will need

+ ¾ yd. (60cm) of a cotton print 60 in. (150cm) wide, or 1 yd. (80cm) of a cotton print 45 in. (115cm) wide

+ ⅜ yd. (30cm) of a solid cotton fabric, 45-in. (115-cm) wide, for the button border

+ three 1 in. (2.5cm) self-cover buttons

+ matching sewing thread

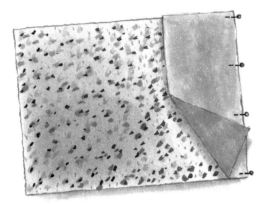

1 Cut two 29¼ x 21¼ in. (74 x 53cm) rectangles from the main fabric for the front and back, and two 9¼ x 21¼ in. (23 x 53cm) rectangles from the border fabric. With right sides together and raw edges even, pin a long edge of one border piece to a short edge of a main piece and machine stitch a ⅝in. (1.5cm) seam. Press the seam toward the border. Join the second border piece to the other main piece in the same way.

2 With right sides together and with the border pieces opened out, pin front to back, aligning the seams. Stitch a ⅝in. (1.5cm) seam along three sides, leaving the border edge open. Trim the corners. Press open the border seams and the next 2 in. (5cm) of the seams on the main pieces. Zigzag the raw edges.

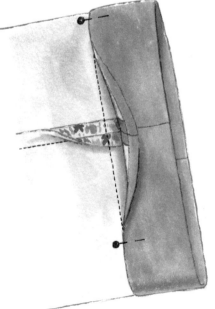

3 Press under a ⅝ in. (1.5cm) seam allowance along the border edge and trim the seam allowance to ½ in. (1cm). Fold the border in half, so that the turned-under edge meets the seam on the wrong side of the pillowcase, and slip stitch in place. Topstitch from the right side close to both edges of the border. Press flat.

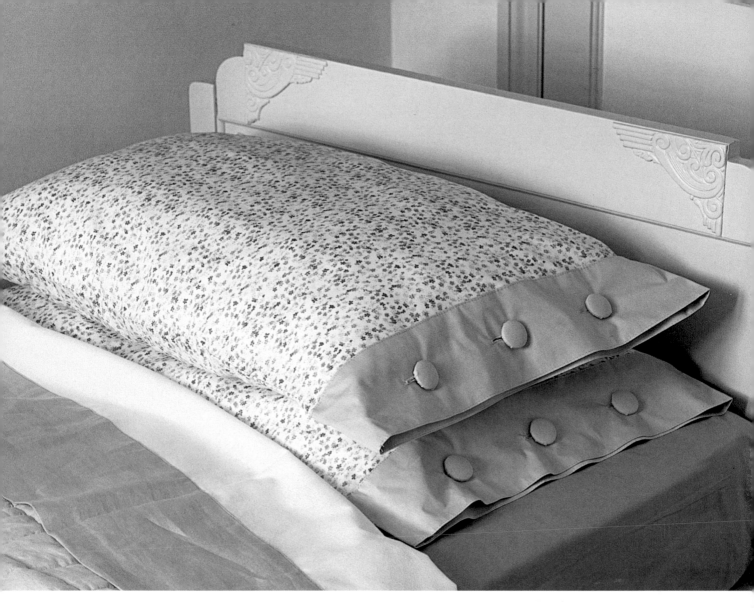

4 Make three evenly spaced buttonholes along the front border, 2 in. (5cm) from the outer edge of the border. Following the manufacturer's directions, cover the buttons in the border fabric and hand sew them to the inside of the back border in line with the buttonholes.

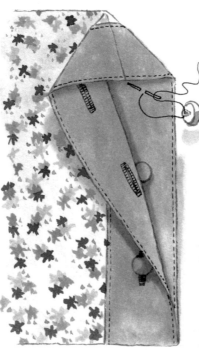

VARIATION

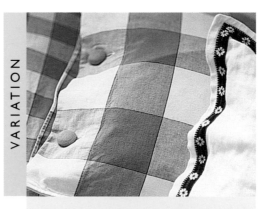

Instead of a plain border and a floral fabric, choose a large check for the whole pillowcase, without a separate band. Cut out two 37¼ x 21¼ in. (94 x 53cm) rectangles and follow the directions from step 2 onward.

jeweled pillow

This sparkling pillow is a wonderful showcase for a collection of rhinestone buckles, brooches, and dress clips. Try hunting in thrift stores and flea markets for anything suitably sparkly. Before making the pillow, clean all the pieces of jewelry with a soft cloth and check that all the paste jewels are fixed. Use small pliers to secure the settings as necessary.

You will need

+ two 20 in. (50cm) squares of fine soft suede or suede-look fabric
+ matching sewing thread
+ 18 in. (45cm) square pillow
+ 19 brooches and buckles
+ dressmaker's fading pen or tailor's chalk
+ low-tack masking tape
+ small pliers

1 Choose one of the larger items to be at the center of the arrangement and place this in the middle of one suede square. Lay seven small buckles in a circle around it. Arrange the remaining pieces around the edge in a circle, leaving a margin of at least 2 in. (5cm) around the outside. The final look will depend on the size and shape of your own jewelry.

2 When you are happy with the arrangement, use a fading pen or tailor's chalk to mark the position of each piece with a couple of tiny dots. Put them down in roughly the same layout on the back panel so that you will remember where they all go.

3 Pin the brooches in place. Hand sew the clips and buckles down with a few stitches using a double length of a sewing thread the same color as the suede.

4 With wrong sides together, attach the front to the back around three sides using tiny strips of low-tack masking tape spaced about 3 in. (8cm) apart. Insert the pillow and tape the remaining side. Carefully machine stitch the front and back together ¾ in. (2cm) from the edge, without stitching through the pillow, and peeling off each piece of tape just before it goes under the presser foot.

Apply the same principles to a different fabric and decorative finish and make the basic pillow from blue denim. A collection of buttons, collected from thrift stores or your granny's button box, can be sewn randomly all over the front of the pillow front to make an informal pillow for a playroom or child's bedroom. You can use your imagination to come up with many different ideas on a similar theme— sequins, badges, beads, or even tassels could all be applied to embellish a plain pillow.

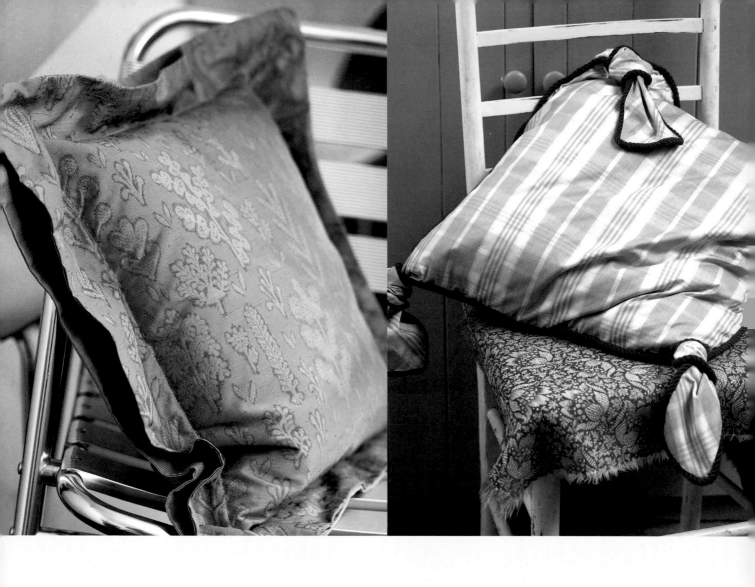

Ruffled & edged
pillows

These are a set of projects with panache. With borders, ruffles, and tassels, these pillows will sit alone in an armchair or nestle beautifully among a set of plainer pillows on a sofa or bed. They demand a little more attention to make, but it's well worth taking the extra time to stitch on a braid or gather a ruffle.

double-flanged border

Two sophisticated woven silk patterns look very stylish with a double flange, giving a glimpse of the contrasting fabric. The texture of the silk lends itself particularly well to this style, which is simple enough that it works just as well in a stronger pattern. The pillow cover is deceptively easy to make, and has a modern feel to it.

You will need

+ 30 in. (75cm) of figured silk, 60 in. (150cm) wide
+ 30 in. (75cm) of plain silk, 60 in. (150cm) wide
+ 18 in. (45cm) square pillow
+ matching sewing thread

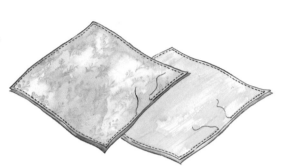

1 Cut four pieces of silk measuring 24 x 24 in. (60 x 60cm), two each from both fabrics. Insure that the grain runs straight and not diagonally, and that the pattern falls neatly. Make one panel by laying two pieces of the same fabric right sides together. Pin and machine stitch them together with a ½ in. (1cm) seam around all four edges, leaving a 4 in. (10cm) opening on one side. Repeat for the other two pieces to make a second panel.

2 Turn the panel right side out and press. Slip stitch the opening. Repeat for the other panel.

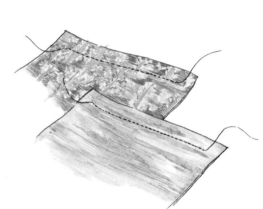

3 On one panel, pin, baste, and machine stitch a line along one edge only, 2½ in. (6cm) from the edge, starting and stopping 2½ in. (6cm) from the adjacent edges. Repeat for the other panel.

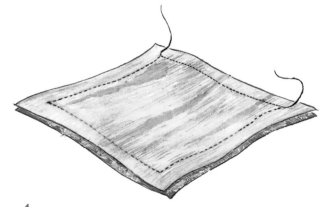

4 Place the two panels on top of each other, lining up the two edges that have the line of stitching. Pin, baste, and machine stitch the three remaining sides through all layers, forming a 2½ in. (6cm) flange all around.

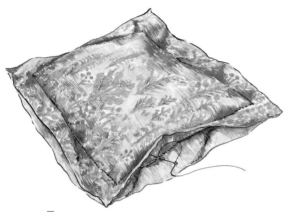

5 Insert the pillow and close the cover inside the two open flaps with slip stitch, following the line of machine stitches.

6 To neaten the corners of the double flange, oversew the four points with a few small hand stitches.

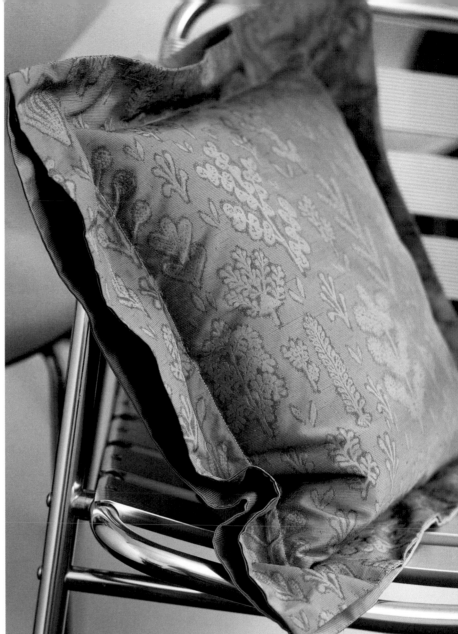

Make a pillow to soften the hard edges of a wooden garden chair by using a sturdy cotton fabric. A pillow with a single flange can be easily made by following the directions for the Tied Pillow Cover (see pages 16–19), but omitting the ties and making the pieces 1½ in. (4cm) bigger all around. After turning the cover right side out and pressing it, topstitch 1½ in. (4cm) from the edges.

double-ruffle taffeta

Silk taffeta has a magical quality to it, and there's no better way to see it than when it is gathered and bunched. Here a tiny checked taffeta is used with a double ruffle effect. The outside ruffle is a single layer of fabric, and the smaller, inside one uses the fabric doubled and tightly gathered, to make a sumptuous pillow.

You will need

+ ¾ yd. (150cm) of checked taffeta, 45 in. (115cm) wide

+ 18 in. (45cm) square pillow

+ 15 in. (38cm) zipper

+ matching sewing thread

1 For the front, cut out one piece of fabric measuring 19 x 19 in. (48 x 48cm). For the back, cut out two pieces measuring 19 x 10 in. (48 x 25.5cm). For the ruffle, cut out two strips, each measuring 4 x 160 in. (10cm x 4m), joining lengths where necessary. To make up the back, place the two pieces right sides together, and along one of the longer edges stitch a 1 in. (3cm) seam, leaving a 15 in. (38cm) gap in the middle. Now baste the gap along the seamline. Press the seam open.

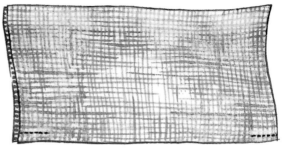

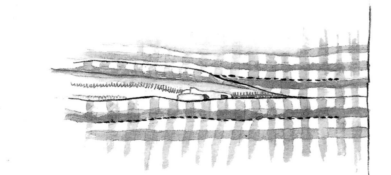

2 On the wrong side of the fabric, center the zipper face down over the opening. Hand baste down both sides of the zipper. With the zipper foot on the machine, topstitch the zipper in place down both sides and across the ends, avoiding stitching through the zipper stops. Remove the basting on the zipper and in the opening. Open the zipper.

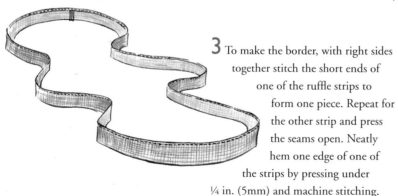

3 To make the border, with right sides together stitch the short ends of one of the ruffle strips to form one piece. Repeat for the other strip and press the seams open. Neatly hem one edge of one of the strips by pressing under ¼ in. (5mm) and machine stitching.

4 Fold the other strip in half lengthwise, wrong sides facing, but do not press the fold. Place the folded strip alongside the right side of the hemmed one and line up the raw edges; baste all the way round, ½ in. (1.5cm) from the raw edges.

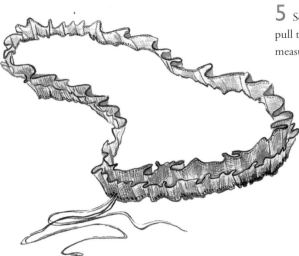

5 Sew a double row of running stitches and pull the threads into even gathers until the ruffle measures 72 in. (180cm).

6 Lay the front piece right side up and place the double ruffle right side down along all four sides, lining up the raw edges. Allow extra fullness at the corners. Pin and baste the border in place ½ in. (1.5cm) from the outside edge.

TIP

When stitching the back to the front, make sure the finished edge of the ruffle isn't caught in the seam. Also, reinforce each corner with another row of stitches 1 in. (2.5cm) to either side of it, on top of the first row.

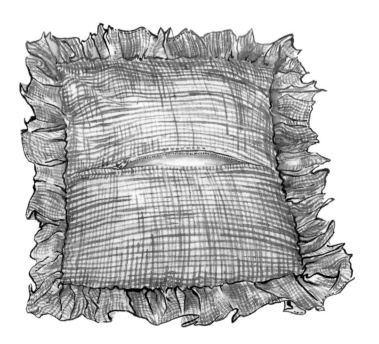

7 Place the back and the front pieces right sides together. Pin, baste, and machine stitch a ½ in. (1.5cm) seam all around the edge, being careful to stitch inside the gathering stitches. At each corner stitch a curve rather than a sharp right angle. Trim the edges and the corners. Turn the cover right side out through the open zipper and insert the pillow.

A double ruffle can be used to decorate a plain pillow if the ruffle is cut
narrower and from a contrasting fabric. This delightful triangular pillow
tucks neatly into the corner of an armchair or sofa, and its unusual shape is
enhanced by the ruffle. Find a shaped pillow first and cut the fabric to fit,
adding a seam allowance all around.

rope-edged knotted pillow

A cool Indian madras cotton is paired with a bright red rope border, sewn directly onto the edge of the cover. The extended corners are long enough to be knotted, to create a fresh and different look. A pile of pillows in inexpensive contrasting madras fabrics can look gloriously exuberant.

You will need

+ 2¼ in. (2m) of cotton fabric, 45 in. (115cm) wide

+ 5½ yd. (5m) of rope edging

+ 18 in. (45cm) square pillow

+ 39 in. (1m) square piece of pattern paper

+ matching sewing thread

+ knitting needle or blunt pencil

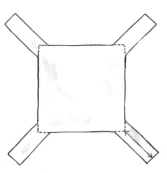

1 Make up a paper pattern in the shape of the pattern shown; the main panel of the cover is 19 in. (48cm) square and at each corner there is an extension or "tail" 10 in. (25cm) long and 3 in. (8cm) wide.

2 Fold the fabric in half, right sides together, matching raw edges. Place the paper pattern on the fabric and pin it in place. Cut out two pieces.

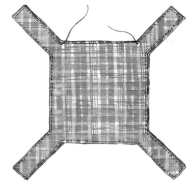

3 Remove the paper pattern. With the fabric pieces still right sides together, pin and machine stitch a ½ in. (1.5cm) seam all around the edge of the panel and the tails, leaving one edge open.

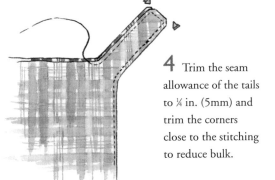

4 Trim the seam allowance of the tails to ¼ in. (5mm) and trim the corners close to the stitching to reduce bulk.

5 With the cover still wrong side out, push a blunt pencil or a knitting needle into the corners of the tails.

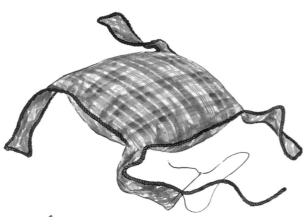

6 Turn the cover right side out and press. Insert the pillow and slip stitch the opening, leaving a small gap to insert the ends of the rope edging. Slip stitch the rope edging in place around the perimeter of the cover, including the tails, and then neatly tuck the ends into the small gap and sew them down.

7 To finish, tie each of the corner tails in a knot. Pull each knot into shape to show off as much of the rope trimming as possible.

VARIATION

Make tassels for a pillow by cutting out four fabric circles. Place a large, round bead in the center of each fabric square, wrap the fabric around it, and tie with strong thread before sewing the tassels to the corners of the pillow.

stripes into squares

A pillow to add a touch of imperial style to a daybed or sofa. Link the material and tassel to other color themes in the room, or perhaps let it stand alone to make a bold statement in what might otherwise be a somewhat dull corner. Here construction and design rely on four triangles mitered together into a square.

You will need

+ 1½ yd. (125cm) of striped cotton, 45 in. (115cm) wide
+ four 7 in. (17.5cm) lengths of thick piping cord
+ decorative tassel
+ 18 in. (45cm) pillow
+ matching sewing thread

1 For the front, cut out four identical fabric triangles, each 21¾ x 15¼ x 15¼ in. (52 x 37 x 37cm), which includes a ½ in. (1cm) seam allowance. The stripes must be the same on each.

2 Place two of the triangles right sides together. Carefully align the stripes and pin, baste, and machine stitch a ½ in. (1cm) seam. Repeat for the other two triangles.

3 Open out and press open the seams. Place the two seamed triangles right sides together, aligning the stripes. Pin and stitch a ½ in. (1cm) seam. Press open the seam, forming a square.

4 For the back, cut out a piece of fabric that is 24 in. (60cm) wide and 28 in. (70cm) long. Fold in half crosswise, press, and cut into two pieces along the fold line.

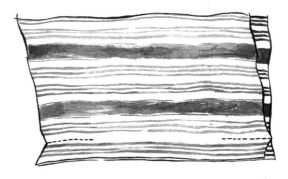

5 Lay the two pieces right sides together. Pin and machine stitch a 2 in. (5cm) seam along one of the long edges, leaving a 14 in. (35cm) gap in the middle. Press the seam open.

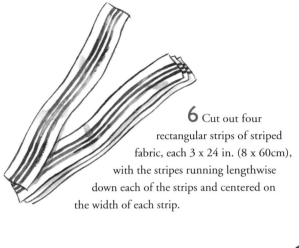

6 Cut out four rectangular strips of striped fabric, each 3 x 24 in. (8 x 60cm), with the stripes running lengthwise down each of the strips and centered on the width of each strip.

7 Right sides together, place a strip along one edge of the back panel. In the same way, lay another strip against an adjoining edge, fold back the corners, pin on the diagonal to form a miter, and press. Pin and machine stitch the miter. Repeat for the other three corners and press.

8 Trim the mitered seam allowances to ½ in. (1cm). Place the mitered border on the back panel, right sides together. Pin and machine stitch a ½ in. (1cm) seam along the outer edge.

9 Turn the border right side out, on top of the wrong side of the back; press. Press under ½ in. (1cm) on the edges of the front panel. With the back wrong side up and the border right side up, lay the front panel right side up on top so it fits inside the border. Pin along the edges of the front panel. Machine stitch very carefully along the edge, stitching through the front, the border, and the back panel. Press.

10 To fasten the back opening, cut out four small squares of the fabric. Turn under ¼ in. (5mm) all around. Cover one end of each piece of cord with a fabric square. Pin the square alongside the back opening as shown. Machine stitch to the back panel without stitching through the front. Knot the other ends of the cords. Sew the tassel onto the front at the center.

VARIATION

Make a cover to coordinate with the Stripes into Squares pillow by using fabric with similar colors. Stitch the four triangles for the front together in the same way, then cut out a square of linen and fray the edges slightly before topstitching it centrally on top. Make up the back as before and join to the front in the same way.

chunky-edged pillow
Piping, fringing, and braid define the edges of beautiful pillows. Home furnishing stores recognize the importance of these finishing touches and are increasingly stocking bigger and better selections of trim styles and colors. Here, a chunky braid makes a bold color statement and adds a contrasting texture to the piece. Match the trim to a color in the fabric to give a simple pillow a luxurious look.

You will need

+ ½ yd. (50cm) of home decorating fabric, 54 in. (136cm) wide

+ 2 yd. (1.8m) of braid

+ 12 in. (30cm) zipper

+ 16 in. (40cm) square pillow form

+ matching sewing thread

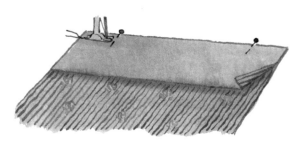

1 Cut one 17¼ in. (43cm) square for the pillow front, and one 17¼ x 14½ in. (43 x 36cm) rectangle and one 17¼ x 4 in. (43 x 10cm) rectangle for the pillow back. With right sides together, pin the large and small pillow back rectangles together along one long edge. Mark 2⅝ in. (6.5cm) in from each end with pins, then machine stitch a ⅝ in. (1.5cm) seam from each end up to the marker pins. Now machine baste the center 12 in. (30cm). Press the seam open.

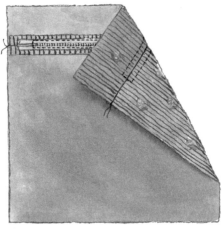

2 Pin the zipper into the basted part of the seam and baste it in place by hand. Using a zipper foot on the machine, stitch the zipper in place from the right side. Remove the basting. Open the zipper.

3 On the right side, pin the braid to the edges of the pillow front along the seam line, with the braid facing inward. Gather the braid slightly at the corners so that there will be enough fullness when the cover is turned right side out, and overlap the ends of the braid by ⅜ in. (1cm). Cut off any excess. Baste the braid in place by hand just within the seam allowance, which is ⅝ in. (1.5cm).

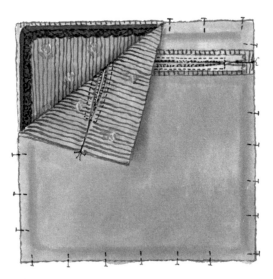

4 With right sides together, pin the pillow front and back together along all four sides, with the braid sandwiched in between. Using a zipper foot and stitching as close to the braid as possible, machine stitch a ⅝ in. (1.5cm) seam along all sides.

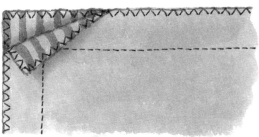

5 Zigzag the raw edges. Remove the basting and turn the cover right side out. Insert the pillow and close the zipper.

The leaves and flowers in this crewelwork design are outlined in dark green and the matching trim emphasizes the effect. A plain pillow can be given endless variations with this simple technique of adding a trim.

ribbon and button lavender pillow Lavender

has been used for centuries to freshen and scent linens, and these lovely pillows, which measure about 6 x 8 in. (15 x 20cm) can easily be slipped into drawers to add a gentle fragrance. They are an effective way of using up small scraps of fabric and are finished beautifully with ribbons, rickrack, and pretty little vintage buttons.

You will need

+ ¼ yd. (20cm) each of two coordinating fabrics
+ ¼ yd. (20cm) each of two coordinating ribbons
+ 1 yd. (80cm) of rickrack
+ matching sewing thread
+ dried lavender
+ small funnel
+ fiberfill stuffing (optional)
+ small buttons

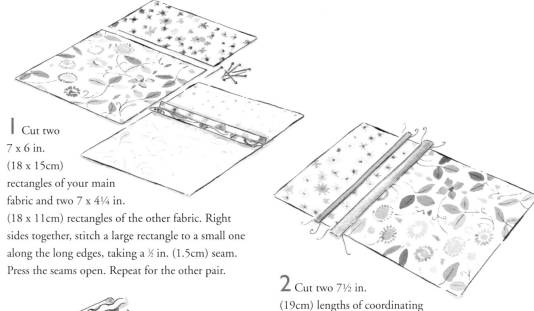

1 Cut two 7 x 6 in. (18 x 15cm) rectangles of your main fabric and two 7 x 4¼ in. (18 x 11cm) rectangles of the other fabric. Right sides together, stitch a large rectangle to a small one along the long edges, taking a ½ in. (1.5cm) seam. Press the seams open. Repeat for the other pair.

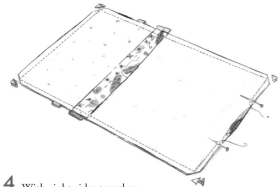

2 Cut two 7½ in. (19cm) lengths of coordinating ribbons. Pin and machine stitch one ribbon along the seam on one piece of fabric, to hide the seam line, and the other about ¼ in. (5mm) from the first, on the narrower section of fabric. Press.

3 Measure and cut a 27 in. (69cm) length of rickrack. Lay the ribbon-trimmed piece of fabric right side up on your work surface. Pin and baste the rickrack all the way around the edge of the fabric, so it is exactly centered over the seam line, which will be ½ in. (1.5cm) from the edge. Ease the rickrack at the corners.

4 With right sides together, lay the second piece of fabric on top of the first. Pin, baste, and machine stitch a ½ in. (1.5cm) seam all the way around the pieces, leaving a gap of about 2 in. (5cm) at one end. Trim the corners and trim the seam allowances to ⅜ in (1cm).

5 Turn the bag the right side out and gently pull the corners out for a neat finish. Press. Fill the bag with dried lavender using a small funnel, or stuff the bag with fiberfill stuffing and add a little dried lavender. Hand sew the opening closed, turning in the seam allowance. Sew buttons onto the ribbon for extra decoration.

VARIATION

Ribbons and rickrack make a pretty way to finish off any vintage-style pillow, but you can find a variety of other braids and edgings in most notions (haberdashery) departments. Look for narrow braids with tiny pompoms, ribbons with fancy edgings, or even a length of old insertion lace that can be stitched into the seams of a pillow made from recycled fabric.

ruffled pillowcase

A contrasting ruffle on a pillowcase creates a soft, romantic look, which you can echo by placing a matching dust ruffle over the base of the bed. Choose a plaid or a check for the main part of the pillowcase, which fits a standard pillow, then pick out one of the colors for the ruffle.

You will need

+ 1 yd. (80cm) of cotton fabric, 54 in. (137cm) wide

+ 1¾ yd. (1.6m) of cotton fabric, 36 in. (90cm) wide, for the ruffle

+ matching sewing thread

1 Cut two 31¼ x 21¼ in. (78 x 53cm) pieces from the main fabric for the front and back and a 9½ x 21¼ in. (24 x 53cm) piece for the flap. From the ruffle fabric, cut two 63 x 7¼ in. (159 x 19cm) strips for the top and bottom ruffles and two 43½ x 7¼ in. (109 x 19cm) strips for the side ruffles. Turn under a ⅜ in. (1cm) hem, followed by a ⅝ in. (1.5cm) hem, along one short edge on the back piece, and machine stitch. Make a hem of the same size along one long edge of the flap piece.

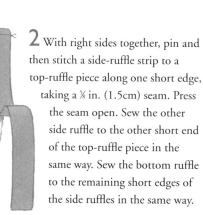

2 With right sides together, pin and then stitch a side-ruffle strip to a top-ruffle piece along one short edge, taking a ⅝ in. (1.5cm) seam. Press the seam open. Sew the other side ruffle to the other short end of the top-ruffle piece in the same way. Sew the bottom ruffle to the remaining short edges of the side ruffles in the same way.

3 With wrong sides together, fold the assembled border in half lengthwise. Baste the raw edges together, and press. Gather the border into a ruffle along the raw (basted) edge, using a double length of thread if you are working by hand or the longest stitch setting on your machine if you are gathering by machine.

VARIATION

For a scalloped border, make the pillowcase 2 in. (5cm) bigger all around and omit the ruffle. After turning it right side out, topstitch all around 2 in. (5cm) from the edge. Now stitch a scalloped embroidery stitch around the edges and then trim just outside the stitching.

4 With raw edges even, pin the ruffle around the edge of the right side of the front, aligning the seams. Gather the ruffle by pulling the gathering threads and baste it in place ½ in. (1cm) from the outer edge.

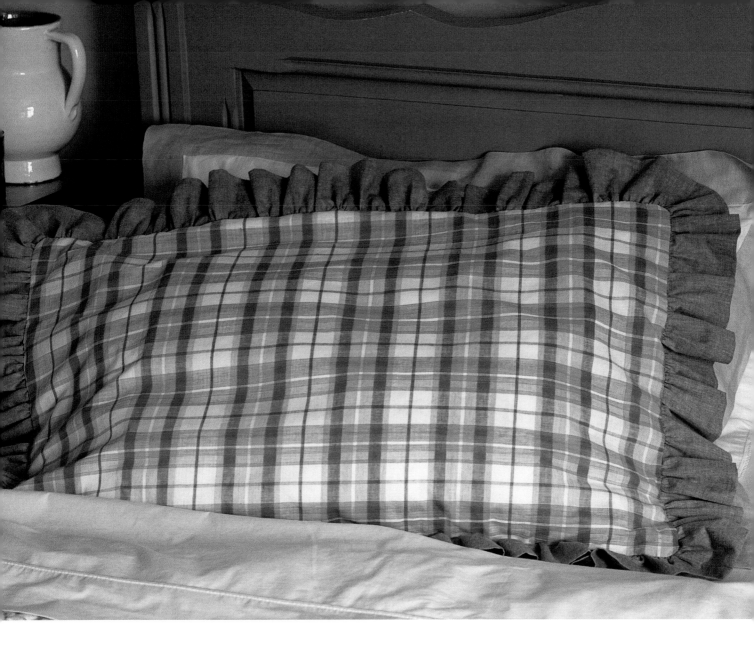

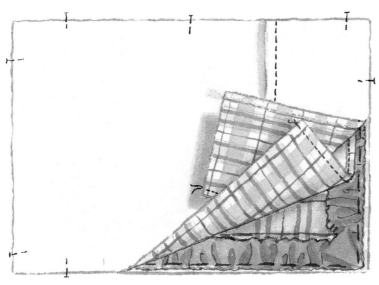

5 With right sides together, pin the back to the front with the ruffled border sandwiched between them and the unhemmed edge of the back piece aligning with one short raw edge of the front. Pin the flap right side down over the hemmed edge of the back piece, with the unhemmed edge of the flap aligning with the other short raw edge of the front piece. Machine stitch around all four sides. Zigzag the edges, trim the corners, turn the pillowcase right side out, and press.

Patchwork
& recycled
pillows

Collecting fabrics and ribbons and piecing them together is a fascinating way to be creative. Patchwork is a traditional craft that developed from the need to conserve every scrap of fabric, and in today's recycling world, it's more relevant than ever. Make a patchwork pillow from favorite fabrics saved from previous projects or use cloth from shirts and dresses no longer worn.

crazy velvet patchwork

Here a puzzle of velvet scraps, some slightly bald and worn, have been pieced together randomly and the joins disguised with decorative feather stitching in a strong color. This is a project to spend time over and to give with love.

You will need

+ assorted colors of velvet to cover the 16 x 18 in. (40 x 45cm) front section

+ 17 x 19 in. (42 x 47cm) piece of velvet, for the back

+ 2¼ yd. (2m) of rope edging

+ embroidery needle and stranded embroidery floss in a contrasting color

+ 16 x 18 in. (40 x 45cm) pillow

+ one sheet each of drawing paper, tracing paper, and thick paper

+ matching sewing thread

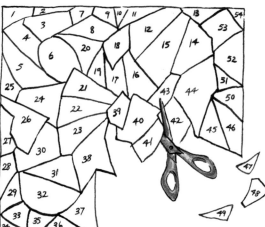

1 To make up the front, sketch an arrangement of crazy-shaped pieces on a 16 x 18 in. (40 x 45cm) sheet of paper. Transfer the design onto thicker paper and give each segment a number before cutting out each shape, then mark the same number on the back.

2 Pin the front face of the shapes to the wrong side of the different colors of velvet and cut them out, adding a ¼ in. (5mm) seam allowance to the fabric around all sides.

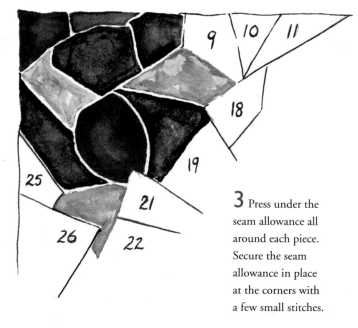

3 Press under the seam allowance all around each piece. Secure the seam allowance in place at the corners with a few small stitches.

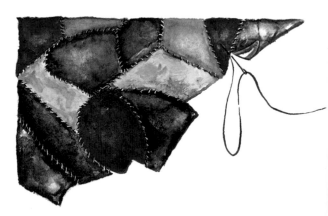

4 Now reconstruct the puzzle design over the original drawing, matching up the numbers segment by segment. Working from the top downward, slip stitch the shapes together, removing the patterns as you join each piece.

5 Once the front section is in one piece, embroider feather stitch (see page 166) over all the seam lines using an embroidery needle and floss.

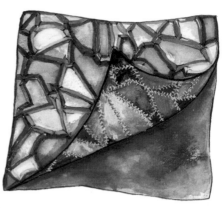

6 Finish the raw edges of the back piece and press under ½ in. (1cm) all around. Lay the front and back sections with right sides together. Hand sew the front and back sections together along three sides using overhand stitch.

7 Turn the cover right side out and insert the pillow. Slip stitch the opening, leaving a small gap.

8 Cut the rope edging to fit the perimeter of the pillow and hand sew it around the edges, feeding the ends of the rope into the small gap before sewing it down for a neat finish.

TIP

This stylish idea would work equally well with a selection of colorful silk scraps, or choose pastel tones for a softer look.

This machine-made version is made from nine identical squares, each consisting of three slanted strips, which are made from three slanted pieces. Make a pattern for the nine pieces in a square, and then cut out nine fabric pieces from each pattern, adding a ¼ in. (5mm) seam around each. Pressing as you go, join the pieces into strips, stitch the strips into squares, and finally join the squares. Add a contrasting border.

fringed pillow with appliqué panel

Fringed with lush cotton and a stylish panel appliquéd to the center, this classic pillow is extremely versatile. The light, fresh-looking colors harmonize well with any decor. Only a small amount of fabric is required for the center panel, which means you can transform a remnant or make a tiny piece of expensive fabric go a long way.

You will need

+ ⅝ yd. (50cm) of home decorating fabric, 54 in. (136cm) wide

+ ¼ yd. (30cm) of fabric, 54 in. (136cm) wide, for the center panels

+ 2¼ yd. (2m) of fringed braid

+ 14 in. (36cm) zipper

+ 18 in. (45cm) square pillow

+ matching sewing thread

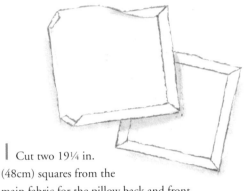

1 Cut two 19¼ in. (48cm) squares from the main fabric for the pillow back and front and two 9 in. (23cm) squares from the second fabric for the center panels. Turn under ⅝ in. (1.5cm) on all edges of the two center panels, trimming and mitering the corners to keep them as flat as possible; baste by hand. With right sides facing up, pin one panel to the center of the pillow front and the other one to the center of the pillow back. Topstitch close to the edges of the center panels.

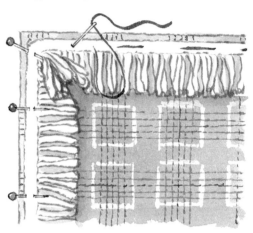

2 Pin the fringed braid to the right side of one of the pillow pieces, with the fringe facing inward. Gather the fringe slightly at the corners so that it will turn the corners neatly when the pillow cover is turned right side out. Baste the fringe in place by hand.

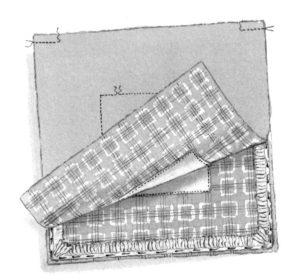

3 With right sides together, pin both pieces together along one edge and machine stitch 2⅜ in. (6cm) in from each end. Now baste the center 14 in. (36cm). Press open the seam.

4 Pin the zipper into the basted part of the seam and baste it in place by hand. Using a zipper foot on the machine, stitch the zipper in place from the right side. Remove the basting. Open the zipper. With right sides together, pin and stitch the remaining edges together with a ⅝ in. (1.5cm) seam. Zigzag the seam allowances. Turn the cover right side out. Place the pillow inside the cover and close the zipper.

You can make any number of variations on this theme, with or without fringing and using different contrast fabrics and colors. It's also a wonderful way to "frame" a floral print in a wide border. This hand-blocked posy is cut from a length of repeated images, isolated on the front of a pillow, and set off by the coordinating stripes of the chair's seat and back.

lavender pillow

Lavender is a highly aromatic plant that has been valued for centuries for its calming properties. A lavender-filled pillow placed in a linen closet not only keeps the linens scented, but also wards off insects. With its floral pattern and dainty bow, this lavender pillow is too lovely to be hidden away, so arrange it with other pillows on a bed and let the delicious aroma tempt you to sleep. A central piece of translucent fabric allows you to glimpse the floral mixture inside.

You will need

+ 10 × 20-in. (25 × 50-cm) piece of cotton fabric

+ 8 × 4-in. (20 × 10-cm) piece of cotton organdy or other translucent fabric such as voile, for the center panel

+ 1 yd. (90cm) length of ribbon, ⅜ in. (1cm) wide

+ 1¼ yd. (1m) of ⅛ in. (3mm) piping cord and a 9 × 11 in. (23 × 28cm) piece of fabric to make the piping, or 1¼ yd. (1m) of purchased piping

+ 7 oz. (200g) of dried lavender flowers

+ small funnel

+ matching sewing thread

1 From the cotton fabric, cut a 9¼ in. (23cm) square for the back, two 3⅞ x 9¼ in. (9.5 x 23cm) rectangles for the front side panels, and two 1⅞ x 4 in. (4.5 x 10cm) rectangles to edge the organdy. To make the center panel, pin one long edge of an edge rectangle to a short edge of the organdy rectangle with right sides together, and machine stitch a ⅝ in. (1.5cm) seam. Trim the seam and press toward the edge rectangle. Stitch the other edge rectangle to the other short edge of the organdy rectangle in the same way.

2 With right sides together, pin a side panel to the center panel along the long edges, and machine stitch. Trim the seam and press toward the side panel. Stitch the other side panel to the other side of the center panel in the same way. Cut two lengths of ribbon the same length as the seam. Pin one on each side of the center panel and topstitch in place, stitching close to the ribbon edges.

3 If not using purchased piping, cut bias strips 1⅝ in. (4cm) wide to make bias binding and make up 1 yd. (1m) of piping (see page 169). Pin the piping around the edge of the right side of the front, clipping into the seam allowances of the piping at the corners and joining the ends where they meet (see page 169). Baste in place. With right sides together, pin the front and back together and machine stitch a ⅝ in. (1.5cm) seam around all four sides, leaving a 3 in. (7cm) gap in one side.

4 Trim the seam, turn the cover right side out, and press. Make a bow from the remaining ribbon and hand sew it onto one of the ribbon stripes. Fill the pillow with dried lavender using a small funnel, and slip stitch the opening.

The same principles for making the lavender pillow apply if you want to make a sumptuous patchwork pillow from brocades and gold ribbon. Join squares into strips, stitch the strips together, and attach ribbon over the seams. A rich tassel trim adds further opulence.

log cabin pillow cover

This is a very traditional patchwork, which takes its name from the log cabins built by the early American pioneers. The central panel was traditionally red, representing the hearth, with the surrounding strips, each of which is longer than the preceding one, forming the logs around it. A selection of red fabrics has been used here, which all complement each other nicely. Experiment with fabrics in lighter and darker tones for a different effect.

You will need

+ selection of fabric scraps at least 2½ in. (6cm) wide and up to 19 in. (47cm) long

+ two 18¾ × 12 in. (47 × 30cm) pieces of fabric for the back of the cover

+ 18 in. (45cm) square pillow

+ matching sewing thread

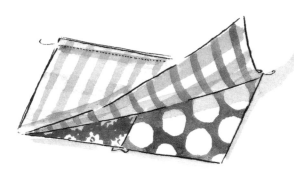

1 Measure and cut a 2¾ in. (7cm) square of one of the fabrics. Make strips of your fabrics 2½ in. (6cm) wide by the width of the fabric. Press all the strips. From one of the strips, cut a piece 2¾ in. (7cm) long. With right sides together, pin and stitch it to one side of the fabric square with a ¼ in. (5mm) seam. Press the seam open.

2 Cut a piece from a different strip, as long as the width of the center square plus the width of the first additional piece. With right sides together, pin and stitch this to the previous two pieces with a ¼ in. (5mm) seam. Press the seam open.

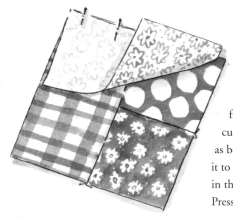

3 Using a strip of fabric in another design, cut a piece for the next side as before and pin and stitch it to the main patchwork panel in the same way as previously. Press the seam open.

4 Cut another piece for the fourth side, which will be as long as the width of the center square plus the two pieces flanking it. Pin and stitch in place as before, and press the seam open.

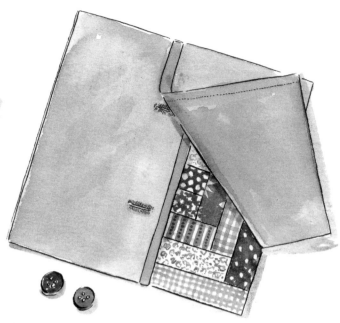

5 Continue to build up
the patchwork adding pieces around it,
making sure that you work in a clockwise direction
without missing out any sides. Increase the length
of the pieces to fit each side until the panel
measures 18¾ in. (47cm) square. Press.

6 For the back of the cover, measure and cut two rectangles of
fabric 18¾ in. x 16 in. (47 x 40cm). Press under ½ in. (1cm)
along one long side of each. Press under another ¾ in. (2cm)
and pin and stitch in place. On one of the pieces make two
buttonholes. Lay this rectangle on the patchwork, right sides
together and raw edges even. Lay the second rectangle on top,
matching up the raw edges, and overlapping the hemmed edges
of the back pieces. Pin and machine stitch a ⅜ in. (1cm) seam
all the way around. Trim the corners and turn right side out;
press. Sew buttons to the underlap, lining them up with the
buttonholes. Insert the pillow and fasten the buttons.

TIP

Many patchwork
and quilting supply
stores (and online
companies) sell
packets of fabrics in
the same weight and
in toning colors, ideal
for projects such as
this. However, a large
part of the fun of
patchwork is selecting
pieces from your own
stash of fabric scraps.

This very simple patchwork idea is made by stitching a vintage
hand-embroidered handkerchief between side panels of floral
cotton. The principle of recycling fabrics holds true, and not
a scrap is wasted.

three-panel patch pillow

This patchwork is called "rail fence" and is made up of blocks of three bars of fabric, which are joined in a nine-patch block. Fabrics of a similar color and tone have been used for a random patchwork, but it can be made with three different-colored fabrics, which can form an attractive zigzag pattern. As with lots of patchwork that is made from square blocks joined together, more blocks can simply be added to fit a larger pillow.

You will need

+ ¼ yd. (20cm) of each of three different fabrics for the patchwork

+ paper for the pattern

+ two 23 × 16 in. (58 × 40cm) pieces of fabric for the back

+ 22 in. (55cm) square pillow

+ matching sewing thread

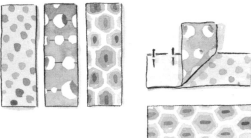

1 Draw and cut out from paper an 8 x 3 in. (20 x 8cm) rectangle. Using this paper pattern, cut out nine rectangles of each of the three fabrics, so you have 27 in total. With right sides together, pin and stitch one rectangle of each fabric together along the long edges with ¼ in. (5mm) seams, varying the sequence. Press the seams open.

2 Continue until there are nine patchwork squares, each made of three rectangles. With right sides together, pin and stitch three of the squares together with a ¼ in. (5mm) seam, arranging them so the first bars are horizontal, the next ones vertical, and the last ones horizontal. Repeat this with the next three squares, but laying the bars vertically this time and then horizontally and finally vertically again. Use the last three squares to create a strip like the first one. Press the seams open.

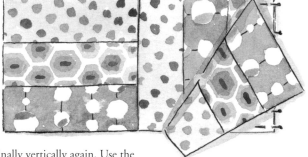

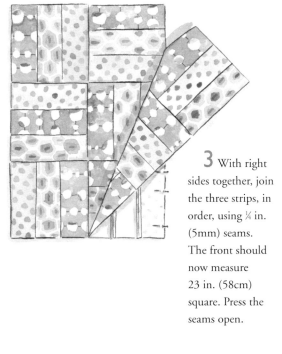

3 With right sides together, join the three strips, in order, using ¼ in. (5mm) seams. The front should now measure 23 in. (58cm) square. Press the seams open.

4 To make the back of the cover, press under ½ in. (1cm) along one long edge of each back piece, then press under another 1¼ in. (3cm). Pin and stitch close to the first fold on both pieces. Place the patchwork panel right side up on the work surface and lay one of the back pieces on it, with right sides together and raw edges even. Place the second back piece wrong side up on top, with the hemmed edges overlapping and raw edges even. Pin and stitch a ½ in. (1.5cm) seam all the way around the cover. Trim the corners and turn the cover right side out. Press. Insert the pillow.

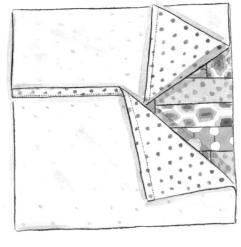

Use remnants or small squares cut from recycled shirts for this traditional-looking patchwork pillow. It's easy to make, but has the look of an old quilt. Follow the directions for the Three-Panel Patch Pillow from step 2 onward, adding a border around the edge if you want one. Make the squares as big or small as you like and go on piecing them together for any size of pillow.

simple patchwork pillow
Mix and match five different fabrics for this quick and easy pillow. As a starter patchwork project it's perfect for beginners because sewing four large squares together really is child's play. In addition, the envelope-style closure at the back means there is no need to insert a zipper or stitch buttonholes.

You will need

+ selection of different cotton fabrics
+ matching sewing thread
+ 18-in. (46-cm) square pillow

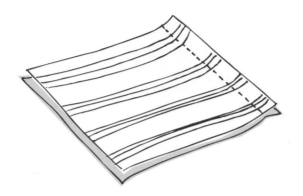

1 From the various fabrics, cut out the pieces for the patchwork front cover: four 8⅝ in. (22cm) squares and four border strips 19¼ x 2¾ in. (49 x 7cm). For the back cover, cut two pieces 19¼ x 13¾ in. (49 x 35cm). With right sides together, pin and stitch two squares together along one side edge, with a ⅝ in. (1.5cm) seam. Repeat with the remaining two squares. Press the seams open.

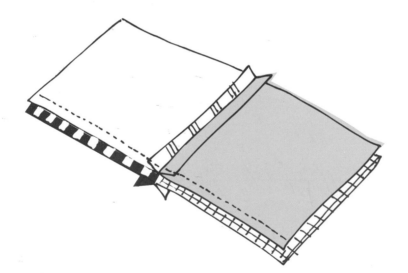

2 With right sides together, pin and stitch the two pairs of joined squares together along one long edge, matching seams and taking a ⅝ in. (1.5cm) seam. Press the seam open.

3 Place one border strip on top of another with right sides together. Pin and baste the strips together at a 45-degree angle from the top corner, stopping ⅝in. (1.5cm) from the bottom edge. Check that the angle is correct, then machine stitch the pieces together along the basted line. Trim the seams and remove the basting stitches.

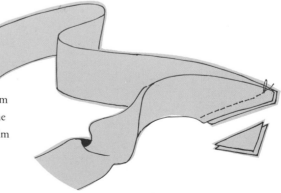

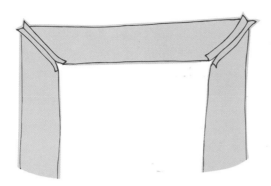

4 Join the other strips together in the same way until the border is complete. Press all the seams open.

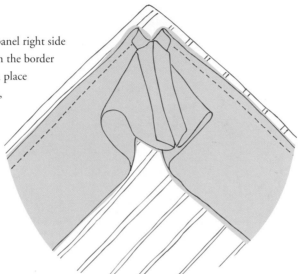

5 Place the square front panel right side up on a flat surface and pin the border to the outer edge. Stitch in place with a ⅝ in. (1.5cm) seam, allowing the seam to open up at the corners. Press the seams open.

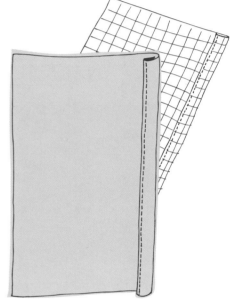

TIP

To stitch a simpler and quicker border on this pillow cover, you could overlap the corners rather than mitering them (as in steps 3 and 4).

6 On one long edge of each back piece, press under ½ in. (1cm) and then a further ½ in. (1cm). Machine stitch the hems in place.

7 Lay the front cover right side up on a flat surface and place the back pieces right side down on top, with raw edges even and the hemmed edges of the back pieces overlapping. Pin and machine stitch the pieces together around the outer edge, taking a ⅝ in. (1.5cm) seam. Trim the corners and turn right side out. Insert the pillow through the back opening.

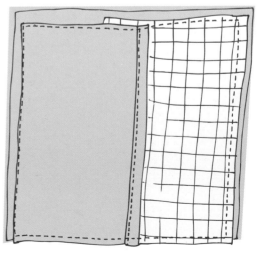

A four-square pillow with attitude! Bold patches made from striped silks running in different directions are combined with zingy striped piping and finished with a covered button in the middle, resulting in a chic, urban pillow. See the Floor Pillow project on page 26 for how to attach the buttons, and page 169 for how to make and attach piping.

nine-block log cabin cover

There are many variations on the basic log cabin patchwork pattern, but they all consist of stitching strips of fabric around a center square, with each strip longer than the preceding one. Traditionally, all the strips are the same width and the center square is twice the width of the strips. In this project, each block is slightly different, which gives you the perfect opportunity to use up tiny scraps of fabric from your stash of thrift store and market finds.

You will need

+ nine 6 in. (15cm) cotton foundation squares

+ scraps of cotton fabric or ribbon in colors of your choice

+ 16 in. (41cm) square of thin cotton to back the patchwork

+ 1¾ yd. (1.6m) piping

+ two 16 × 10½ in. (41 × 26.5cm) pieces of linen

+ matching sewing thread

+ two large buttons

+ 15 in. (38cm) square pillow

1 To work out the position of the first piece of fabric, draw diagonal lines from corner to corner across a foundation square, taking care not to stretch the fabric. Place the center square right side up in the middle of the foundation square, aligning the corners with the drawn diagonal lines.

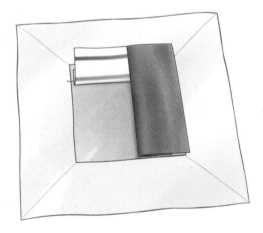

2 The width of all strips should be half that of the square. The first strip should be the length of the square. (It's best to cut each strip slightly longer than you need and trim it once you have stitched it in place.) Place the strip on top of the center square, right sides together, and baste it in place.

3 Machine stitch the strip to the center square, fold the strip back to the right side, and press with your fingertips or a warm iron so that the strip lies flat.

4 The length of the next strip should be the length of the center square plus the width of the first strip. Stitch it to them in the same way.

5 Still progressing around the square in a clockwise direction, add two more strips, increasing the length of each strip as you go.

6 Add more "rounds" of four strips each until the foundation square is full and the block complete.

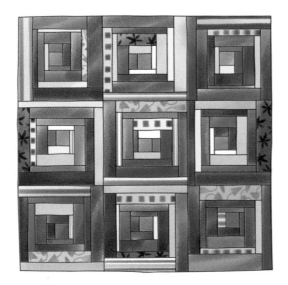

7 Make nine blocks in total, and stitch them together in three rows of three, taking ½ in. (1cm) seams. Press the seams to one side. Sew the completed patchwork to a piece of backing fabric—thin cotton is ideal.

8 Following the directions on page 169, make enough piping to go around the pillow. Pin, baste, and machine stitch the piping to the right side of the front, ½ in. (1.5cm) from the edge, with the raw edges of the piping facing outward.

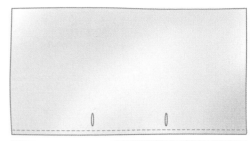

9 Trim off any excess fabric around the corners, making sure you don't cut into the piping. Trimming makes the corners of the cover less bulky so that the pillow will fit neatly inside.

10 Make a ½ in. (1cm) hem along one long edge of each back piece. Make two buttonholes on the hemmed edge of one piece, 1 in. (2.5cm) from the edge.

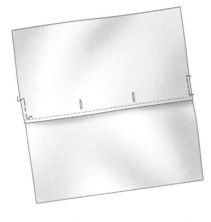

11 With both back pieces right side up and the buttonholes on top, overlap the edges so the back is the size of the front. Baste together at the sides. Right sides together, stitch the back to the front, following the stitching line of the piping.

VARIATION

12 Turn the cover right side out, and sew the buttons to the underlap of the back in line with the buttonholes on the overlap of the back. Insert the pillow and fasten the buttons.

Create a more contemporary variation of log cabin patchwork by using a toile de Jouy fabric for the center square and making a few wider strips cut from checks or other patterned fabrics. The spiraling design of log cabin patchwork is not used in this variation, but the principle of joining strips outward from a center square is the same.

pillowcase with patterned border This

crisp, white cotton pillowcase has a cheerful and colorful fabric border. You could use the same fabric to edge sheets, as well—a simple way to create a really special wedding or housewarming gift.

You will need

+ ½ yd. (50cm) of patterned fabric

+ ⅛ yd. (10cm) of solid-color fabric

+ 21 in. (53cm) length of ribbon, ¼ in. (5mm) wide

+ 1⅛ yd. (1m) of white fabric

+ matching sewing thread

1 Cut a 21 x 16 in. (53 x 41cm) piece of patterned fabric and two 21 x 3 in. (53 x 7cm) pieces of solid-color fabric. With right sides together and raw edges even, lay one solid-color strip along each long edge of the patterned fabric. Pin and stitch ½ in. (1.5cm) seams; press open. On the right side, stitch ribbon over one seam.

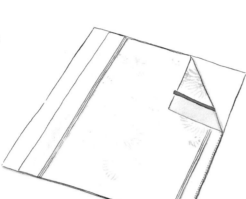

2 Cut a 21 x 21¼ in. (53 x 54cm) piece of white fabric. With right sides together, pin the border piece to the white fabric, with the ribbon-edged piece closest to this seam. Stitch a ½ in. (1.5cm) seam. Press the seam toward the border piece.

3 At the other end of the border, press under ½ in. (1.5cm). With wrong sides together, fold the border back on itself and hand sew in place, aligning the turned-under edge with the seam stitched in the previous step. Press.

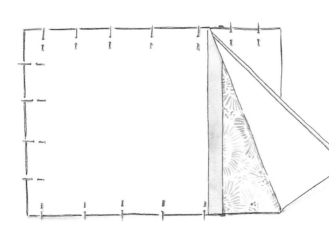

4 Cut a 21 x 38½ in. (53 x 98cm) piece of white fabric. Along one short end, press under ⅜ in. (1cm) and then another ½ in. (1.5cm). Machine stitch, stitching as close to the edge as possible. Lay the piece right side up on your work surface. Lay the front of the cover right side down on top, aligning the raw edges. Fold the hemmed flap of white fabric over the front of the cover. Pin and stitch a ½ in. (1.5cm) seam along the short raw end and both long sides. Trim the seams and turn right side out. Press.

Patching different fabrics together and covering the seams with ribbon is the ideal way to recycle vintage fabrics or use scraps left over from previous projects. Use the best parts of a worn-out summer dress or blouse or a much loved child's dress. The combination of colors and patterns is endless, and it's a wonderful way to be creative.

transfer print pillow
Instead of keeping family photos tucked away in albums, transfer the images onto fabric and make them into pillows to keep for yourself or give as nostalgic presents. These covers feature black-and-white snapshots, with borders made from 1960s fabric. Most copy shops can reproduce photographs on fusible transfer paper, which is available from stationery stores if you want to print digital images from a computer.

You will need

+ solid-colored fabric (to coordinate with the patterned fabric)
+ patterned fabric
+ old photograph
+ plain white cotton fabric
+ matching sewing thread
+ two buttons (optional)
+ 15 x 19 in. (38 x 48cm) pillow form

1 The measurements given here are for a 6 x 10 in. (15 x 25cm) picture and a 15 x 19in. (38 x 48cm) rectangular pillow; adapt them as necessary to fit the proportions of your own photograph and form.

From solid-colored fabric cut out the following:
For the inner border: two 2 x 6 in. (4.5 x 15cm) strips and two 2 x 12 in. (4.5 x 30cm) strips
For the outer border: two 2 x 14 in. (4.5 x 35cm) strips and two 2 x 20 in. (4.5 x 50cm) strips
For the back: one 2½ x 16 in. (6 x 40cm) strip

From patterned fabric cut out the following:
For the main border: two 4 x 8 in. (9.5 x 20cm) strips and two 4 x 18 in. (9.5 x 45cm) strips
For the back: two 12 x 16 in. (30 x 40cm) rectangles

2 Transfer your image onto the white cotton fabric and trim it down to 6 x 10 in. (15 x 25cm). With right sides together, pin and machine stitch the short solid-colored inner border strips to the short sides of the picture using a ½ in. (1cm) seam. Press the seams outward, using a pressing cloth so the iron doesn't touch the transferred image. Attach the two long inner borders to the long edges of the picture in the same way.

3 With right sides together, pin and machine stitch the short, then the long, patterned strips to the inner border with ½ in. (1cm) seams. Press seams inward.

4 To complete the front panel, add the short and long outer border strips in the same way, pressing the seams outward.

5 To make the back, press under ½ in. (1cm) along one long edge of the remaining colored strip. Matching the raw edges and with right sides together, pin and stitch the strip to one of the patterned back rectangles along one long edge using a ½ in. (1cm) seam. Press the strip outward, then press it in half lengthwise and fold it over to bind the raw edge. Pin and stitch just inside the seam. If using buttons, make two buttonholes, 6 in. (15cm) from each side (see page 167). Make a narrow double hem along one long edge of the remaining rectangle.

6 To assemble the cover, pin the bound rectangle to the top of the front panel with right sides together and raw edges even. Pin the other rectangle with raw edges even and the finished edges of the two back panels overlapping. Baste the three pieces together at the edges, then machine stitch. Trim the corners, turn right side out, and press. Insert the pillow and secure the opening with a few slip stitches, and a couple of buttons if you wish.

Use the same method of overlapping strips to frame a panel of embroidered fabric. Here, four wide strips of blue and white striped fabric contrast with a central panel featuring a bright splash of red.

Shaped
pillows

Who said pillows had to be rectangular? Heart shapes, cubes, circles, or triangles can all be made into quirky pillows for adding something a little different to a room. Children will love the triangular floor pillows with appliqué animal faces, and the set of pretty bolsters will bring country style to any room. For more sophisticated style, choose from one of the round pillows that are buttoned and corded or trimmed with pompoms.

heart-shape pillow

This delightful heart-shape pillow could grace any room in the home. Shown here on a kitchen chair painted to match one of the colors in the pillow fabric, it would look equally at home on a solid-color sofa or a crisp cotton waffle bedspread.

You will need

+ brown paper for patterns
+ dressmaker's fading pen or tailor's chalk
+ 13 × 28 in. (33 × 71cm) of lining fabric
+ feathers, fiberfill stuffing, or other stuffing of your choice
+ 14 × 29 in. (36 × 74cm) of fabric for cover
+ matching sewing thread
+ snaps

1 For the heart pattern, fold a 12 × 27 in. (31 × 69cm) piece of brown paper in half lengthwise and draw one half of a heart shape. Open out the pattern, place it on one half of the lining fabric, and draw around it with a soft pencil (this will be the stitching line). Cut out two pieces of lining fabric, cutting ½ in. (1cm) outside the drawn line.

2 Right sides together, pin and machine stitch the two lining-fabric hearts together, stitching along the drawn line, leaving a 4 in. (10cm) gap on one side. Trim the corners and clip into the seam allowance on the curves, taking care not to cut through the stitching. Turn right side out, stuff to the desired fullness, and slip stitch the gap closed.

3 Make a pattern for the cover that is 1 in. (2.5cm) larger all around than the pillow pattern. Fold in half, then fold a generous overlap. Cut one piece from fabric for the front, using the full pattern. Fold the pattern to the overlap and cut two back pieces from the fabric. Mark the center foldline on each back piece using a fading pen or tailor's chalk.

4 Press under and machine stitch a narrow double hem on the raw straight edge of each back piece. Place the back pieces on the front piece, right sides together and raw edges even, and machine stitch all around the outside edge taking a ½ in. (1cm) seam. Turn the cover right side out, sew snaps along the opening, and insert the pillow.

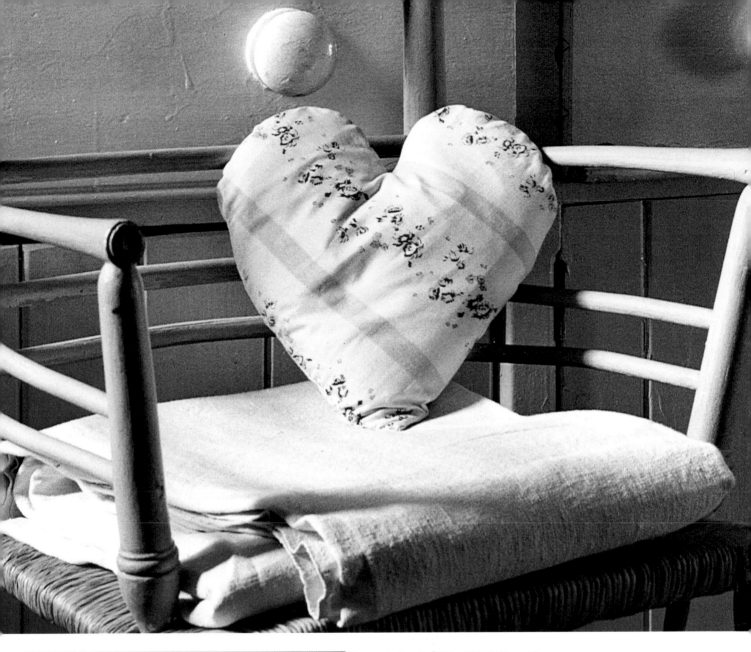

VARIATION

The heart shape came originally from the folk art of Eastern Europe and is still a very popular motif. Fill a small fabric heart with dried lavender and hang it in a closet or sew it to the front of a pillow, as pictured here. Make a paper pattern and cut out two pieces (you could use pinking shears if you wish, as the raw edges are visible). Stitch the pieces with wrong sides together, leaving a small gap. Fill with dried lavender before slip stitching the gap. Sew a vintage button to the top.

buttoned round pillow This elegant round pillow
looks equally good among other shapes or on its own on the seat of an
upholstered occasional chair. The buttoned center pulls the cover in to give
an attractive, plumped-up effect. Remove the buttons before laundering the
cover, or simply dry clean the pillow.

You will need

+ ¾ yd. (70cm) of home
  decorating fabric, 54 in.
  (136cm) wide

+ ½ yd. (50cm) of contrasting
  fabric, 54 in. (136cm) wide,
  for the piping and covered
  buttons plus 3½ yd. (3m)
  piping cord, or 3½yd. (3m)
  readymade piping

+ 14 in. (36cm) zipper

+ two 1½ in. (38mm)
  self-cover buttons

+ 18 in. (45cm) round pillow
  with sides 2 in. (5cm) deep

+ matching sewing thread

+ upholstery needle and
  extra-strong sewing thread

1 From the main fabric, cut two 19¼ in. (48cm) circles for the
pillow front and back and two 31 x 3¼ in. (80 x 8cm) rectangles
for the boxing strip (gusset). If you are making your own
piping, prepare 3½ yd. (3m)—see page 169. Pin
the piping around the edges on the right side of
both circles, with the piping raw edges facing
outward and the piped edges inside the
seamline. Cut notches in the piping seam
allowance to ease it around the curves, and
join the ends of the piping together (see
page 169). Baste in place.

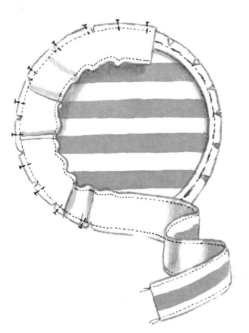

2 Right sides together, stitch the two boxing strips
together along one short edge; press open the seam.
Stitch down both long edges of the strip ⅜ in. (1cm)
from the edges. Right sides together, pin one long
edge of the strip around the edge of one of the
circles, clipping the seam allowance of the strip up
to the stitching so it will follow the curve.

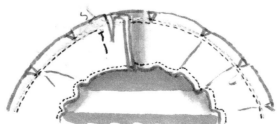

3 Allowing a ⅝ in. (1.5cm)
seam allowance on each end,
cut off any excess fabric at
the point where the short
ends of the boxing strip meet.

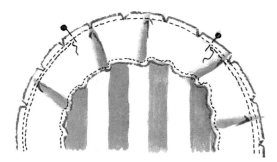

4 Measure 14 in. (36cm) along the seamline and mark with pins to leave an opening for the zipper. Machine stitch along the seam line and machine baste between the pins. Press open the seam.

5 Pin and hand baste the zipper into the basted part of the seam. Using a zipper foot on the machine, stitch it in place from the right side. Remove the hand and machine basting. Open the zipper. Right sides together, machine stitch the short ends of the boxing strip together.

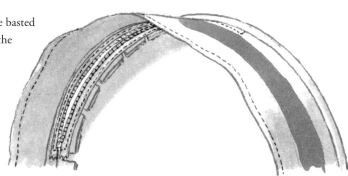

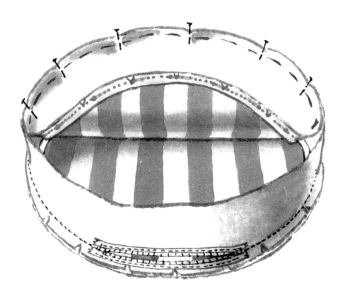

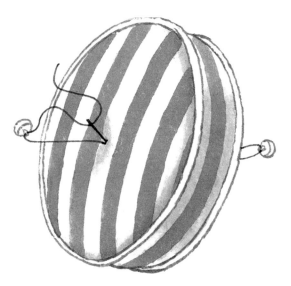

6 Right sides together, pin the other long edge of the boxing strip to the other circle, clipping up to the stitching line to follow the curve. Machine stitch the pieces together. Zigzag the raw edges and turn the cover right side out.

7 Place the pillow inside the cover and close the zipper. Following the manufacturer's directions, make two covered buttons to match the piping fabric. Using extra-strong thread and an upholstery needle, sew one button on the front and one on the back, stitching back and forth between them through the center of the pillow, pulling tightly. Tie a knot securely to fasten.

Make a softer version of the round pillow by giving it the same treatment as the Mattress Cushion project (pages 144–146). Catch stitch around the edge and button it with five tufts on each side.

pompoms

Round cushions are readily available, though they are often quite flat. This large, thick size can lend itself to both traditional and modern decor. Here a creamy dotted muslin looks almost ethereal with the addition of two rows of cotton pompom fringe. This looks simpler to make than it is—just follow the steps carefully.

You will need

+ 1¾ yd. (1.5m) of dotted muslin fabric, 60 in. (150cm) wide

+ 2¾ yd. (2.5m) of piping cord

+ 2¾ yd. (2.5m) of pompom fringe

+ 15 in. (38cm) round cushion, 4 in. (10cm) deep

+ matching sewing thread

+ basting thread in a contrasting color

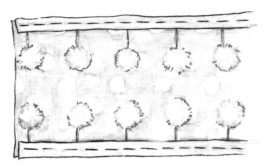

1 For the top and bottom of the cover, cut out two circles of fabric, each with a diameter of 18 in. (45cm). For the boxing strip (gusset) cut out a strip measuring 5 x 49 in. (13 x 123cm). Place the strip right side up. Cut the length of fringe in half and pin and baste a length of fringe along each of the long edges of the boxing strip on the right side, matching the raw edges.

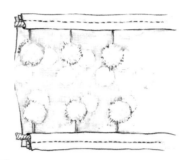

2 Next make the piping by cutting out the two lengths of fabric on the bias (see page 169) each measuring 1 x 49 in. (2.5 x 123cm). Make up two lengths of piping (see page 169). Lay the piping over the fringe so that the raw edges of the piping face outward. Pin the piping along the seam line, ½ in. (1cm) from the edge. Baste and machine stitch through all layers. Repeat for the other long edge of the boxing strip.

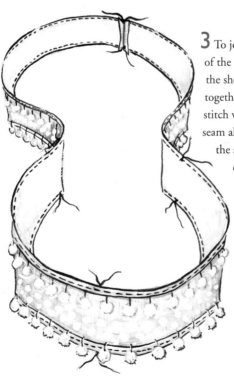

3 To join the open ends of the side strip, place the short ends right sides together and machine stitch with a ½ in. (1cm) seam allowance. Press open the seam. On both long edges, use hand stitches in a contrasting thread to mark points a quarter, a half, and three quarters of the way around the seam.

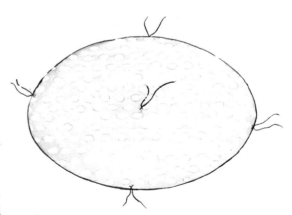

4 For the main body, fold each circle of fabric into quarters and mark the center point with a contrasting-colored stitch, then mark the quarter points on both the perimeters in the same way.

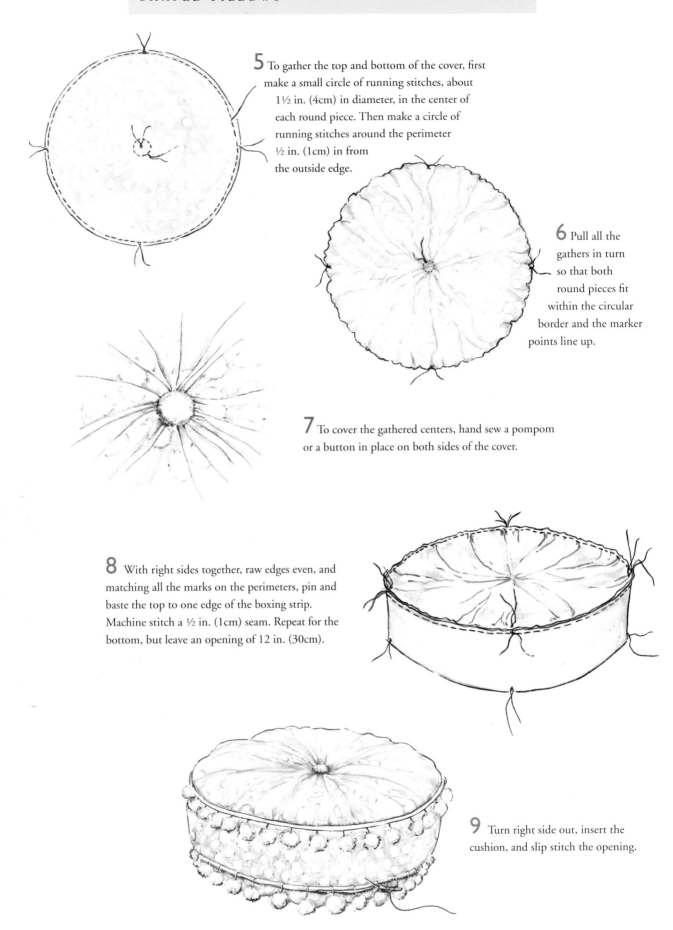

5 To gather the top and bottom of the cover, first make a small circle of running stitches, about 1½ in. (4cm) in diameter, in the center of each round piece. Then make a circle of running stitches around the perimeter ½ in. (1cm) in from the outside edge.

6 Pull all the gathers in turn so that both round pieces fit within the circular border and the marker points line up.

7 To cover the gathered centers, hand sew a pompom or a button in place on both sides of the cover.

8 With right sides together, raw edges even, and matching all the marks on the perimeters, pin and baste the top to one edge of the boxing strip. Machine stitch a ½ in. (1cm) seam. Repeat for the bottom, but leave an opening of 12 in. (30cm).

9 Turn right side out, insert the cushion, and slip stitch the opening.

Round pillows make a good contrast to the familiar rectangle, and a set of rectangular pillows can be given a lift with the addition of a round one thrown down beside them. If you are working with a variety of shapes, restrict your color choice to two or three. These pillows, both ruffled and round, are pulled together by the strong, two-color fabrics. Piping in the solid color accentuates this, as well as defining the shapes.

ottoman

There is something very satisfying about creating a piece of furniture from scraps of fabric! This patchwork ottoman is made from a nine-patch panel on the top with side panels of six squares; a solid square of fabric is stitched onto the bottom (although you could make another nine-patch panel following the steps for the top) and then the cover is filled with stuffing. Try recycling old blankets or woolens for a more vintage look, or use squares of corduroy in different colors to striking effect.

You will need

+ 24 in. (60cm) squares of each of four wool fabrics

+ 20 in. (50cm) square of fabric for the base

+ paper for pattern

+ 39 x 53 in. (100 x 135cm) of stiff fusible interfacing

+ fiberfill stuffing

+ matching sewing thread

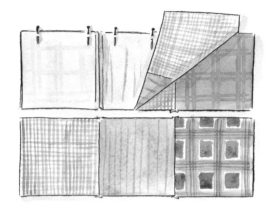

1 Draw a 6¾ in. (17cm) square on paper and cut out to use as your pattern to cut 33 squares of fabric (eight each of three fabrics and nine of one). Take nine of the squares and arrange them in three rows of three, making sure that no two squares of the same fabric are next to each other. With right sides together, pin and stitch three of the squares together using ¼ in. (1cm) seams to form a strip.

2 Repeat this with the other six squares to form three strips of three squares. Press seams open. Right sides together, pin and stitch these strips together with ¼ in. (1cm) seams to form a square. Press seams open. Following the manufacturer's directions, iron stiff interfacing to the back of this panel.

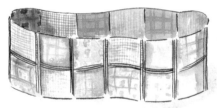

3 Join more squares together in this way to make four panels of six squares. Iron stiff interfacing to the wrong side of each panel. With right sides together, join these panels together with ¼ in. (1cm) seams to form a long strip two squares deep and 12 squares long. Join the ends together to form a loop.

4 With right sides together and raw edges even, pin and stitch this loop onto the patchwork square, lining up the seams and matching the vertical joins on the sides to the corners of the square.

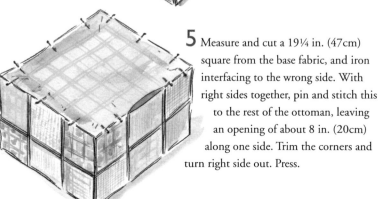

5 Measure and cut a 19¼ in. (47cm) square from the base fabric, and iron interfacing to the wrong side. With right sides together, pin and stitch this to the rest of the ottoman, leaving an opening of about 8 in. (20cm) along one side. Trim the corners and turn right side out. Press.

6 Stuff the ottoman, pushing the stuffing into all the corners to form a neat cube. Pack the stuffing firmly in for a more solid ottoman, or use slightly less for a saggier look. Slip stitch the opening closed.

VARIATION

Instead of a square ottoman, make a round one with two circles and a long strip. This one has been made with a boldly striped fabric, but you could make a patchwork version by stitching wide strips of contrasting fabrics together.

silk brocade bolster cover

This multicolored silk brocade bolster cover is an exercise in unashamed extravagance, guaranteed to add a touch of boudoir-like luxury to even the most ordinary surroundings. The lustrous brocade cover is trimmed with ribbon or braid, and it is piped and gathered at each end. Matching covered buttons at the ends complete the opulent effect.

You will need

+ silk brocade in dark turquoise, lime green, and pink

+ two 23 in. (58cm) lengths of woven ribbon or braid

+ two 23 in. (58cm) lengths of medium piping cord

+ 18 x 6½ in. (45 x 16cm) bolster

+ two 1¼ in. (3cm) self-cover buttons

+ matching sewing thread

1 For the main cover, cut out one 7 x 23 in. (18 x 58cm) strip of dark turquoise silk, one 5½ x 23 in. (14 x 58cm) strip of lime-green silk, and one 9 x 23 in. (23 x 58cm) strip of pink silk. For the gathered ends, cut two 4½ x 23 in. (11 x 58cm) strips of lime-green silk. For the piping, cut two 2 x 23 in. (5 x 58cm) bias strips of pink silk, cut with diagonal ends sloping in the same direction. With right sides together, pin and baste the three strips of silk together to make the cover. Machine stitch a ⅝ in. (1.5cm) seam. Press the seams open. Pin the two lengths of braid to the right side, covering the seams. Baste and machine stitch in place, starting both lines of stitching from the same end to prevent the braid puckering.

2 With right sides together, pin, baste, and machine stitch the shorter edges to make a cylinder, taking a ⅝ in. (1.5cm). Press the seam open and turn the cover right side out.

3 Join the ends of one length of piping cord together to form a loop (see page 169), overlapping them by ⅝ in. (1.5cm). Sew the diagonal ends of one bias strip with right sides together, taking a ⅝ in. (1.5cm) seam; press the seam open. Wrap the fabric over the cord with wrong sides together and pin and baste close to the cord. Make the second round of piping in the same way.

4 Matching the raw edges and lining up the seams, pin and baste a round of piping around each end of the main cover, allowing for a ⅝ in. (1.5cm) seam allowance.

5 With right sides together, join the short edges of an end strip with a ⅝ in. (1.5cm); press the seam open. Press under ⅝ in. (1.5cm) around one edge; stitch. With right sides together and raw edges even, slip the end loop over one end of the main cover, covering the piping and lining up the seams. Pin and baste, then machine stitch a ⅝ in. (1.5cm) seam using a zipper foot or piping foot. Do the same at the other end with the other end strip.

6 Insert the bolster and, using a double length of thread, work a round of long running stitches around one opening slightly less than ⅝ in. (1.5cm) from the hemmed edge. Pull the thread up gently to form evenly spaced gathers. Tuck the hem inside the cover and knot the ends of the gathering threads tightly; do not cut. Finish off the other end in the same way. Following the manufacturer's directions, cover the buttons with scraps of pink fabric; sew them in place at each end. When the cover needs cleaning, cut off the buttons, snip the thread, and remove the pad.

Bolsters are subject to many interpretations. One idea is to make simple round, flat ends instead of gathering them. The ends of this silk bolster have been machine embroidered with a spiral of contrasting thread and decorated with a flamboyant tassel. If you are making this variation, leave a gap in the side seam before inserting the bolster and then slip stitch the opening to close.

ribbon-tied bolster cover

A bolster adds an interesting decorative touch to a sofa, as well as adding an extra degree of comfort. This bolster cover is made by joining strips of fabric to form a panel, which is then stitched to cover the bolster. The design means that there is no need to sew a zipper or buttons and buttonholes onto the cover, because the drawstring ends make it simple to remove the cover for laundering.

You will need

+ 18 x 24 in. (45 x 60cm) piece of main fabric

+ 4 x 24 in. (10 x 60cm) piece of each of three coordinating fabrics

+ fabric for piping

+ 48 in. (120cm) length of piping cord

+ two 22 in. (55cm) lengths of ribbon, ¼ in. (5mm) wide

+ 18 x 7 in. (45 x 17cm) bolster

+ matching sewing thread

+ safety pin

1 Measure and cut a 11½ x 22 in. (29 x 56cm) rectangle of main fabric. Cut two 2¼ x 22 in. (6 x 56cm) strips of one of the coordinating fabrics. With right sides together, pin and stitch a strip onto either side of the main piece of fabric with ⅜ in. (1cm) seams; press open.

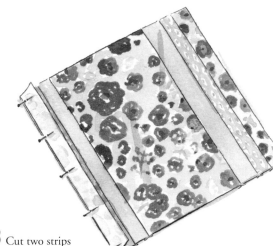

2 Measure and cut two strips of a second coordinating fabric 1¾ x 22 in. (4.5 x 56cm). With right sides together, pin and stitch a strip onto either side of the main panel with ⅜ in. (1cm) seams, pressing the seams open.

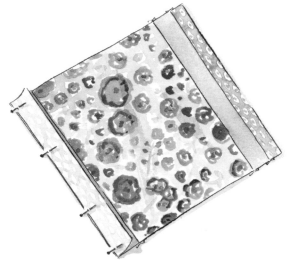

3 Cut two strips measuring 1¾ x 22 in. (4.5 x 56cm) from the third coordinating fabric. Again, with right sides together, pin and stitch a strip onto either side of the main panel using ⅜ in. (1cm) seams, and press the seams open.

4 Following the directions on page 169, make two lengths of piping, each 23½ in. (59cm) long. Lay these along each end of the patchwork panel and baste in place with the basting ⅜ in (1cm) from the edge. Cut two 4¾ x 22 in. (12 x 56cm) strips of the main fabric . With right sides together, pin and stitch these along the edges using the zipper foot or piping foot on your machine, insuring that the stitching sits snugly against the piping. Press open.

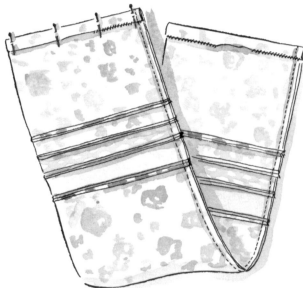

5 Fold the patchwork panel in half lengthwise with right sides together, and pin and stitch a ⅜ in. (1cm) seam along the longest side, forming a tube.

6 Press under ½ in. (1cm) at each end of the fabric tube and press. Press under another ½ in. (1cm), and pin and slip stitch in place, leaving a gap of about ⅝ in. (1.5cm) in the stitching.

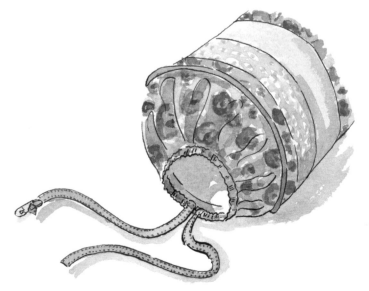

7 Attach a safety pin through one end of one of the ribbons and push it through the channel at the end of the fabric tube until it comes back out through the hole. Remove the safety pin and pull the ribbon to gather the fabric. Tie the ends of the ribbon in a bow. Push the bolster into the cover and thread the ribbon through the other end, again finishing with a bow.

Country cottons make comfy bolster covers for an armchair when they are used in conjunction with soft, warm blankets or throws. For a cover like the one shown here, make a long roll with a dotted fabric and attach contrasting facings at both ends. After inserting the bolster, secure the ends with ties made from the contrasting fabric (see pages 28 and 32–34 for how to make the ties).

pyramid beanbag

An endearing gingham cat and rabbit smile out from these bright pyramid floor pillows. The fleece covers are quick to remove and washable, while the inner pads, filled with polystyrene beads, are squashy and warm. They are lightweight enough for children to drag easily around the house. Always use a pressing cloth when ironing fleece or it will melt.

You will need

+ 24 × 48 in. (60 × 120cm) rectangle of fire-resistant interlining

+ bag of fire-resistant polystyrene beads

+ fusible bonding web

+ 10 in. (25cm) square of cotton gingham

+ scrap of contrasting gingham

+ 24 × 48 in. (60 × 120cm) rectangle of knitted fleece fabric

+ scraps of main fleece and of contrasting fleece or felt

+ colored chalk pencil

+ matching and contrasting sewing thread

+ two buttons for the eyes

+ 20 in. (50cm) nylon zipper

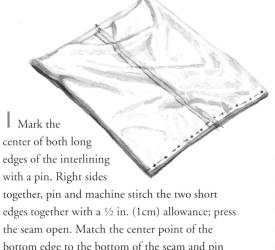

1 Mark the center of both long edges of the interlining with a pin. Right sides together, pin and machine stitch the two short edges together with a ½ in. (1cm) allowance; press the seam open. Match the center point of the bottom edge to the bottom of the seam and pin the two edges together to make a bag. Baste, then machine stitch a ½ in. (1cm) seam.

2 Pin the top edge together in the opposite direction, starting at the seam and leaving an 8 in. (20cm) gap at the end for filling. Machine stitch a ½ in. (1cm) seam, then turn the lining right side out. Press under the seam allowance along the gap.

3 Using a mug as a scoop, fill the lining three-quarters full with polystyrene beads, leaving enough empty space for it to squash down. Pin the opening closed, then machine stitch across the seam.

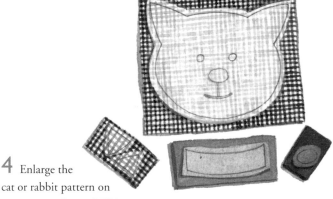

4 Enlarge the cat or rabbit pattern on page 173 as directed. Using a pencil, trace the main outline, the inside ears, collar, and nose onto the paper side of the fusible web. Cut them out, leaving a narrow margin around each shape. Following the manufacturer's directions, iron the face onto the large piece of gingham, the ears onto the gingham scrap, the collar onto the fleece scrap, and the nose onto a scrap of the main fleece. Cut out each piece around the outline. Iron the face centrally to the fleece rectangle, then add the ears, nose, and collar. Draw the mouth using a chalk pencil.

Make a stylish doorstep by making a smaller version of the Pyramid Beanbag project and using a heavier filling inside it, such as dried peas. This is a good way to use up smaller pieces of fabric. You could also add a small ribbon loop as in the picture above.

5 Thread the sewing machine with thread to match the gingham, and satin stitch around the face and collar to conceal the raw edges. Sew around the nose and ears in the main color and add the mouth in black. Sew on the two buttons for the eyes.

6 Mark the center of the two long edges of the fleece rectangle with a pin. With right sides together, pin and baste the short edges together with a ¾ in. (2cm) seam. Machine stitch the seam for 2 in. (5cm) at each end, then press the seam open. Insert the zipper. Remove the basting and open the zipper. Join the top and bottom of the cover as for the interlining (see steps 2–3). Turn right side out, insert the beanbag, and close the zipper.

Embellished
pillows

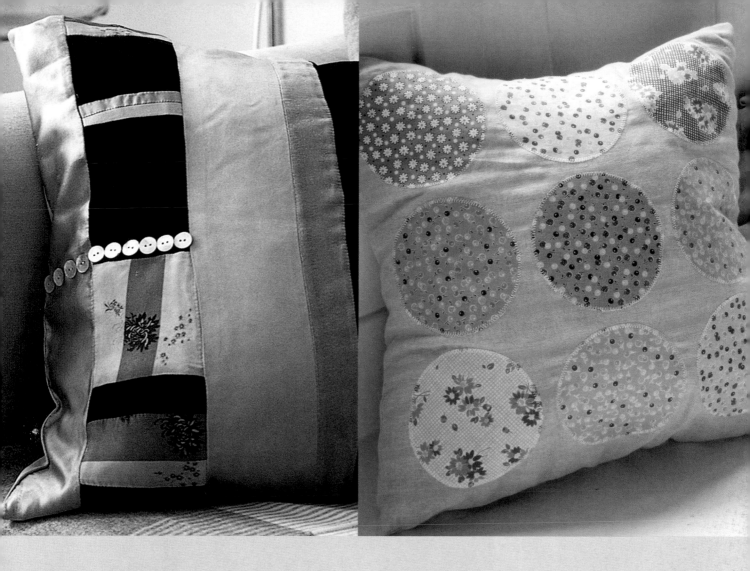

Once you are familiar with pillow-making techniques, it's time to start decorating them with ribbons, embroidery, or appliqué, and these pillows are luxurious and ornamented. Beginners might like to get going with the easy monogrammed pillow, but if you have the skill and the time nothing could be more rewarding than making one of the more elaborate pillows for a special gift.

silk & satin stripes

Despite its long heritage and historic tradition, a patchwork pillow doesn't have to be homespun or folksy. This refreshingly modern version is pieced using opulent satins, brocades, and velvets. The contrasting textures and skillful choice of colors give it a sumptuous appearance, which is completed with a row of iridescent pearl buttons.

You will need

+ a selection of luxury-fabric remnants, such as grosgrain, velvet, silk brocade, and satin

+ 22 in. (55cm) square of matching fabric for back

+ matching sewing thread

+ ten ½ in. (1cm) pearl buttons

+ transparent nylon sewing thread

+ 22 in. (55cm) square pillow

1 Cut out the following 23 in. (57cm) long strips: gray grosgrain 6½ in. (16cm) wide; deep red velvet 7 in. (17cm) wide; blue brocade 3½ in. (8cm) wide; pinky-beige satin 5½ in. (13cm) wide; blue satin 4½ in. (11cm) wide. For the patchwork strip, cut out a selection of 13cm (5in) wide pieces of different lengths. Lay the small pieces of fabric for the patchwork strip in a row, varying the colors and lengths. With right sides together, pin and machine stitch ½ in. (1cm) seams, until the strip measures 23 in. (57cm) long. Press each seam lightly to one side, toward the thicker fabric, using a pressing cloth to protect the material.

2 With right sides together, pin and machine stitch the first four strips from step 1 together along their long edges with ½ in. (1cm) seams. Press the seams as before.

3 Join the patchwork strip to the edge of the fourth strip, then join the remaining long strip to the patchwork strip to form a 23 in. (57cm) square. Press the seams toward the patchwork strip.

4 With right sides together, pin the front and back covers together. Machine stitch around all four edges with a ½ in. (1cm) seam, leaving a 19 in. (47cm) opening in one side. Trim the corners.

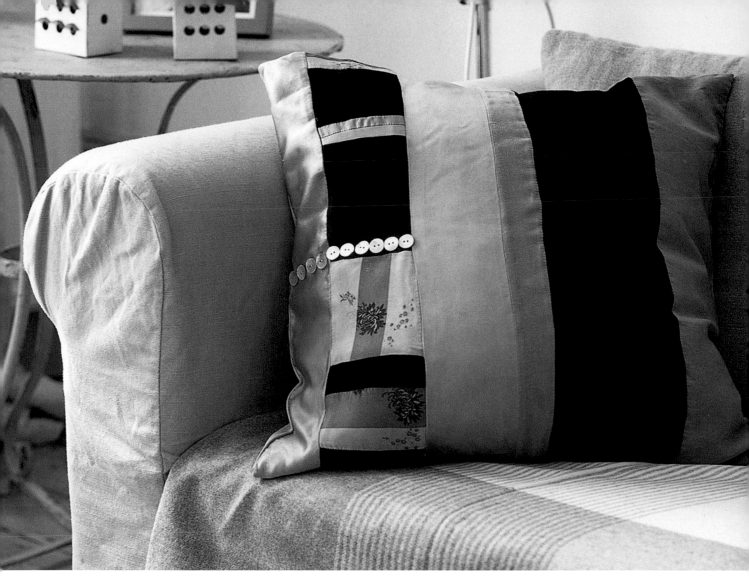

5 Press under the seam allowances of the opening. Turn the cover right side out and press the edges lightly. Using invisible nylon thread, sew the buttons onto the cover in a row, from the inside edge of the patchwork strip to the outside edge of the cover. Insert the pillow. Slip stitch the opening closed.

VARIATION

Using strips in different directions is the basis of the Silk & Satin Stripes pillow, but this technique can be used to make an assortment of different pillow designs and effects. Using coarse-weave fabric in two colors produces a more homespun pillow, which fits in well with a contemporary monochrome interior that relies on texture rather than color.

initials in cross stitch

What could be more personal than embroidering someone's initials into a pillow design? Cross stitch is extremely simple and gives lovely results. Here the cream edging on the scallops is echoed in the embroidery. When you have decided on the initials you wish to stitch, make an accurate chart to refer to and count rigorously; the pattern is on page 170.

You will need

+ ½ yd. (50cm) of brown evenweave linen, 44 in. (115cm) wide

+ 12 x 18 in. (30 x 45cm) piece of cream felt

+ cream stranded embroidery floss

+ 9 x 18 in. (23 x 45cm) rectangular pillow

+ graph paper and pattern paper

+ embroidery needle and hoop

+ drawing compass

+ pinking shears

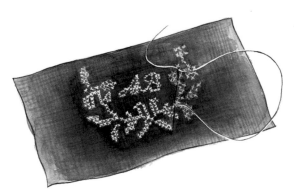

1 Cut two 10 x 19 in. (25 x 47cm) pieces of linen and use one of these pieces as a base for the cross-stitch decoration. Trace the pattern onto graph paper and then transfer it to the center of the fabric. Place the fabric in an embroidery hoop, and embroider the design in cross stitch (see page 170) using cream floss and an embroidery needle.

2 To make the scalloped edges, cut one strip of brown linen measuring 6 x 19 in. (15 x 47cm) and two strips of felt measuring 6 x 18 in. (15 x 45cm). Make a pattern on a 3 x 19 in. (8 x 47cm) piece of pattern paper. Draw four part-circles along the top of the paper with a 4¾ in. (11.75cm) diameter. Mark a point 1½ in. (4cm) from the bottom edge between each circle; draw a straight line through the points. To make the scallops, cut out the outline of the top half of each circle.

3 Fold the linen strip in half lengthwise, wrong sides together. Lay the pattern over it, lining up the long straight edge with the long raw edges of the fabric, and pin it down. Cut out the shapes, remove the paper, and clip between the scallops. Turn under ½ in. (1cm) along the curves and the two short ends of the strips and press.

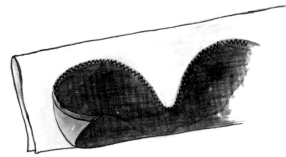

4 Fold the felt strips in half lengthwise and place a scalloped linen piece on top of each one. Pin, baste, and zigzag stitch the pieces together along the edge of the linen around the scallops and the short ends.

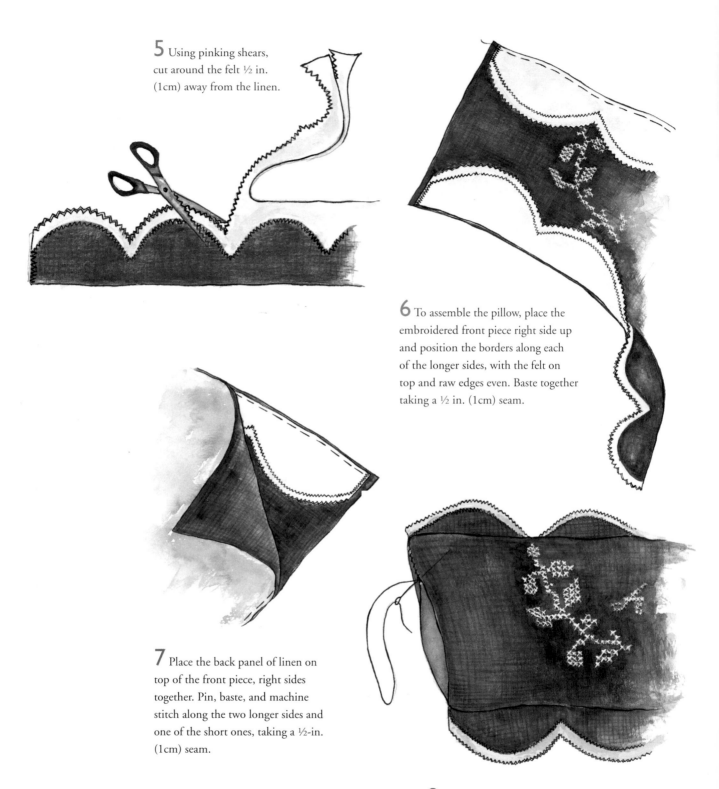

5 Using pinking shears, cut around the felt ½ in. (1cm) away from the linen.

6 To assemble the pillow, place the embroidered front piece right side up and position the borders along each of the longer sides, with the felt on top and raw edges even. Baste together taking a ½ in. (1cm) seam.

7 Place the back panel of linen on top of the front piece, right sides together. Pin, baste, and machine stitch along the two longer sides and one of the short ones, taking a ½-in. (1cm) seam.

8 Turn the cover right side out; press. Insert the pillow. Slipstitch the opening closed.

If you love embroidery, use your passion to create an embellished pillow using wool fabric and yarns such as crewel yarn for a warm, chunky pillow that's perfect for a winter living room. Cut out two rectangles slightly bigger than the pillow and draw your basic design straight onto the piece of fabric for the front. Embroider the design and then stitch this piece to the back of the cover in the usual way.

autumnal appliqué

Like many other forms of needlecraft, appliqué has survived for generations and lends itself particularly well to all manner of designs, pictorial or abstract. All you need to do is decide on a motif, or series of motifs, draw and cut them out from scraps of fabric, then apply them to a background. There is a pattern for the leaves on page 171.

You will need

+ ⅝ yd. (50cm) of heavy cotton fabric, 45 in. (115cm) wide

+ ¼ yd. (25cm) of contrasting fabric for the motif, 45 in. (115cm) wide

+ 18 in. (45cm) square pillow

+ ¼ yd. (25cm) fusible bonding web, 45 in. (115cm) wide

+ tracing paper

+ matching sewing thread

1 Cut out two pieces of the heavy cotton fabric, each measuring 19 x 19 in. (48 x 48cm), for the front and back panels. Make sure the grain of the fabric is straight. Take the piece of contrasting fabric and iron it smoothly onto the fusible web and cut out four rectangles to fit the leaf motifs (see page 171).

2 Draw the shapes of the appliqué leaf motifs on the tracing paper, increasing the proportions to the desired size. Cut them out, and lay them over the contrasting fabric squares. Secure them in place with pins and carefully cut out each leaf.

3 Remove the paper and iron the leaves to the right side of one of the cotton pieces. Machine stitch them in place, close to the edges, using a straight stitch.

4 To decorate the leaves, machine stitch the outline of the veins and the stalks in a different colored thread using a tight zigzag stitch.

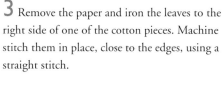

5 To assemble the pillow cover, lay the remaining piece of cotton over the appliquéd piece, with right sides together and raw edges even. Pin, baste, and machine stitch a ½ in. (1cm) seam along three sides of the cover.

6 Turn right side out, insert the pillow, and slip stitch the open end closed.

VARIATION

For an instant appliqué pillow, make the cover following steps 1–3 and step 5. Cut out the leaves following the picture (left), omitting the decorative stitching, and do not top stitch the leaves after ironing them in place.

monogrammed pillow

This is a wonderful way to personalize a handmade pillow cover. A monogrammed item incorporating the initials of the recipient or an anniversary date is very special and makes a thoughtful gift that will be treasured. The simplest way to obtain letters is from a computer—scale up the required initials, print, and cut out, then use these as your pattern. Felt is the easiest fabric to use as it does not ravel.

You will need

+ rectangular piece of antique linen fabric two and a half times the depth of the pillow, by the width of the pillow, plus 1¼ in. (3cm) for seam allowances

+ square pillow

+ felt square

+ matching sewing thread

+ traced or computer-printed, initial or lettering

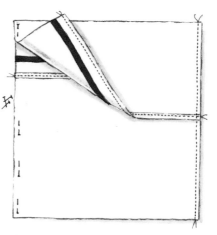

1 Press under a ⅜ in. (1cm) double hem down both short ends of the fabric. Machine stitch in place.

2 With right sides together, fold the fabric crosswise into a square shape to fit the size of your pillow, overlapping the hemmed ends at the center. Pin and machine stitch the sides together with ⅝ in. (1.5cm) seams. Trim corners. Turn right side out and press.

3 Using your traced or printed lettering as a pattern, cut out the letters from the felt and arrange on the front of the cover. Pin in place. Hand sew the lettering in place, making sure you don't catch the back cover with the stitching as you sew. Insert the pillow through the back opening.

VARIATION

For a more permanent monogram, embroider a cross stitch letter (see pages 116 and 170) onto a square of linen in a contrasting color—red on white is a classic combination. Fray the edges of the square by removing threads parallel to each edge, teasing them out with a pin, and stitch it to the front of a gingham pillow before you make it up.

4 If you need to launder your cover frequently, it may be best to make your lettering detachable, as some felt is not colorfast when laundered. The best way to do this is use small pieces of Velcro tape hand-sewn to the letters and to the front of the cover, to fasten the letters in place.

polkadot appliqué pillow
Stitch large circles of patterned fabric onto plain linen to make this delightfully dotty pillow cover. Choose scraps of your favorite fabrics for the circles and edge them with a small zigzag stitch to prevent them from fraying.

You will need

+ selection of scraps of patterned fabrics

+ ⅝ yd. (50cm) natural-colored linen

+ 18 in. (45cm) square pillow

+ 14 in. (35cm) zipper

+ matching sewing thread

+ fusible bonding web (optional)

+ compass and paper for pattern

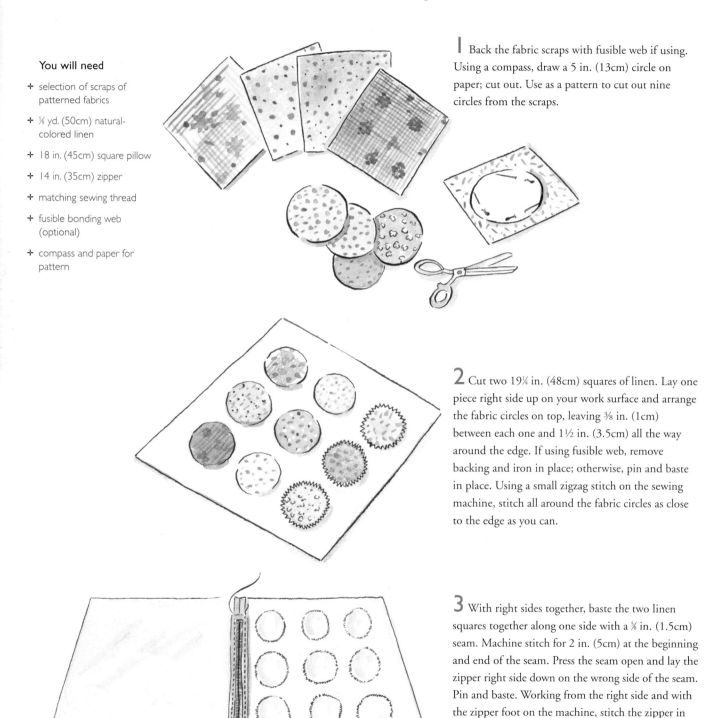

1 Back the fabric scraps with fusible web if using. Using a compass, draw a 5 in. (13cm) circle on paper; cut out. Use as a pattern to cut out nine circles from the scraps.

2 Cut two 19¼ in. (48cm) squares of linen. Lay one piece right side up on your work surface and arrange the fabric circles on top, leaving ⅜ in. (1cm) between each one and 1½ in. (3.5cm) all the way around the edge. If using fusible web, remove backing and iron in place; otherwise, pin and baste in place. Using a small zigzag stitch on the sewing machine, stitch all around the fabric circles as close to the edge as you can.

3 With right sides together, baste the two linen squares together along one side with a ⅝ in. (1.5cm) seam. Machine stitch for 2 in. (5cm) at the beginning and end of the seam. Press the seam open and lay the zipper right side down on the wrong side of the seam. Pin and baste. Working from the right side and with the zipper foot on the machine, stitch the zipper in place. Remove the basting. Open the zipper.

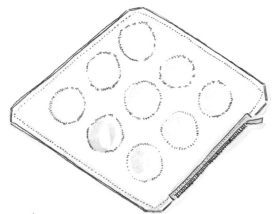

4 With right
sides together and raw edges even, pin and machine
stitch along the remaining three edges with a ⅜ in.
(1.5cm) seam. Trim the corners and turn the cover
right side out. Press. Insert the pillow.

If you have a computer-
aided sewing machine, you
will be able to machine
embroider your own
circles on the pillow front
before you stitch the front
to the back. Use a selection
of colors that are in close
harmony with each other
to make subtle variations
within the circles. Adding
a darker circle every so
often adds depth to the
design and creates a
punchier effect.

beribboned pillow
This is the perfect way to use up all those leftover bits of ribbon that never seem to be quite long enough to be useful. Collect together ribbons and braids in similar colors and stitch them onto plain fabric to make a stylish pillow cover that no one would guess was made from scraps.

You will need

+ ½ yd. (40cm) of solid-color fabric, 45 in. (115cm) wide

+ selection of ribbons in harmonizing colors and various widths

+ matching sewing thread

+ 14 x 20 in. (35 x 50cm) pillow

+ three buttons

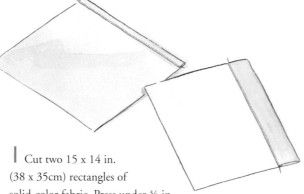

1 Cut two 15 x 14 in. (38 x 35cm) rectangles of solid-color fabric. Press under ⅜ in. (1cm) along one long edge of each piece. Press under another ½ in. (1.5cm) on one piece and 2 in. (5cm) on the other piece. Machine stitch both hems close to the edge.

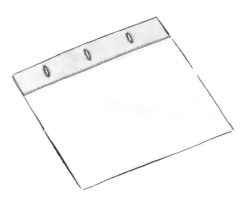

2 Make three buttonholes along the wider hem to fit the size of the buttons you are using.

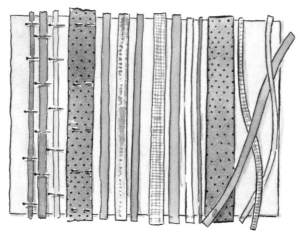

3 Cut a 15 x 21 in. (38 x 53cm) rectangle of solid-color fabric. Lay it on your work surface and place the ribbons on the right side of the fabric. When you are happy with the arrangement, pin and hand baste them in place, then topstitch along both long edges of each ribbon. Remove the basting stitches.

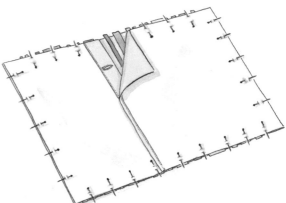

4 Lay the ribbon-covered piece right side up on your work surface, and the buttonholed back piece right side down on top, aligning the raw edges. Place the other back piece right side down on top, again aligning the raw edges, and pin in place. Machine stitch a ½ in. (1.5cm) seam around the edges, trim the corners, and turn right side out. Press. Sew three buttons onto the underlap of the back, in line with the buttons. Insert the pillow and fasten the buttons.

This is such an easy idea, and it's one that is perfect for a young girl's bedroom. A set of decorative pillows makes her bed into a daybed if piled up on top of the pillows. Vary the theme with a strip of flowery fabric in the center flanked by ribbons in all her favorite colors.

ribbon weave

This sumptuous woven-ribbon pillow works on the simple principle of basket weaving. Seven different shades of velvet ribbon are cut into equal lengths and woven across the surface of the pillow. This idea can be adapted using just two colors for a checkerboard design or even just one color to create a textural effect.

You will need

+ ⅝ yd. (50cm) of velvet fabric, 45 in. (115cm) wide

+ ⅝ yd. (50cm) of thin interlining fabric

+ seven different colors of velvet ribbon, 1 in. (2.5cm) wide, with a total length of 20 yd. (18m)

+ 2¼ yd. (2m) of velvet piping

+ four tassels

+ 18 in. (45cm) square pillow

+ 14 in. (35cm) zipper

+ matching sewing thread

1 To create the ribbon effect on the front, cut 19½ in. (49cm) strips from each color of ribbon. It does not matter if there are more strips of some colors—this will add to the effect. Cut out a piece of interlining fabric 19 in. (48cm) square. Pin the strips face up along one edge of the interlining, leaving ½ in. (1cm) free of ribbon at each side. Try to achieve a random effect with the colors. Baste and machine stitch along the top of the ribbons to secure them, ½ in. (1cm) from the edge.

2 Starting from the top, weave the remaining ribbons horizontally, threading them under and over the vertical ribbons. Alternate the colors to create a random pattern and anchor them to the sides with pins. Push each ribbon tightly against the one above.

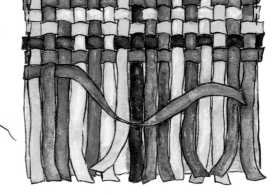

3 Continue interweaving the ribbons until the interlining is covered and then baste the three loose sides down.

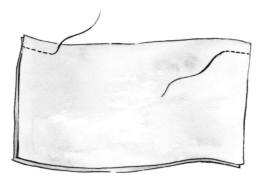

4 For the back, cut out two pieces of velvet measuring 19½ x 10 in. (48 x 25 cm). Place the panels right sides together and along one of the longer sides machine stitch a 2 in. (5cm) seam, leaving an opening of 14 in. (35cm) in the center. Baste the opening. Press the seams open.

TIP

Secure the ribbon strips while you weave them by pinning the top strip onto a firm surface like an ironing board. As each horizontal strip is woven, pin it onto the interlining beneath.

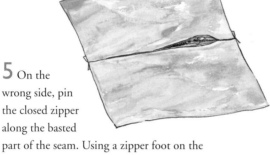

5 On the wrong side, pin the closed zipper along the basted part of the seam. Using a zipper foot on the machine, stitch the zipper in place from the right side. Remove the hand and machine basting. Open the zipper.

6 Lay the velvet piping around the perimeter of the back piece on the right side, with the raw edges of the piping facing outward. Pin and baste them together with the stitching line ½ in. (1.5cm) from the edge of the fabric.

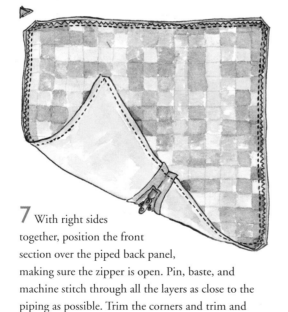

7 With right sides together, position the front section over the piped back panel, making sure the zipper is open. Pin, baste, and machine stitch through all the layers as close to the piping as possible. Trim the corners and trim and finish the raw edges to prevent raveling.

8 Turn the cover right side out, insert the pillow, and close the zipper. Sew a tassel to each corner with small hand stitches.

Use this easy ribbon-weaving technique to decorate a variety of household projects. Different widths of ribbons or braids, or even strips of felt (which doesn't ravel), can be attached to an interlining backing and made up into a bolster or a chair seat cover. Varying widths of ribbon will give different effects, so experiment with the way that narrow and wide can be used in conjunction with each other. Your choice of color will also have a major impact on the look, whether you go for subtle harmonies or strong clashes.

yo-yo pillow

This is the perfect introduction to simple sewing. The yo-yos are made from scraps of patterned fabric, sewn onto a store-bought cover to create an inexpensive but very decorative pillow. If you're making a pillow in a different size, remember that the finished yo-yos will be about half the size of the original circle. It's also best to make all the yo-yos from the same weight of fabric; lightweight dress cotton is ideal.

You will need

+ 10 in. (25cm) lengths of a selection of small-patterned fabrics

+ paper for pattern

+ compass

+ matching sewing thread

+ store-bought pillow cover to fit 14 in. (35cm) square pillow

+ 14 in. (35cm) square pillow

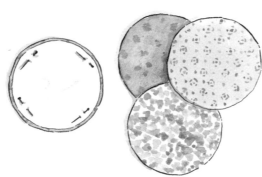

1 Using a compass, draw a circle 4¾ in. (12cm) in diameter on paper. Cut out and pin the template onto your fabric. Cut out 36 circles from a variety of fabrics. Press under ¼ in. (5mm) all the way around.

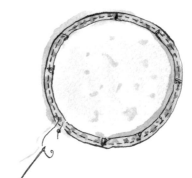

2 Hand sew a line of running stitches around each circle close to the fold. Pull the thread to gather, and secure with a few stitches.

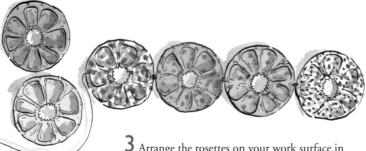

3 Arrange the rosettes on your work surface in six rows of six, making sure that no two rosettes of the same fabric are next to one another. Hand sew each row together with a few small stitches, and then sew the six rows together in the same way to form a panel.

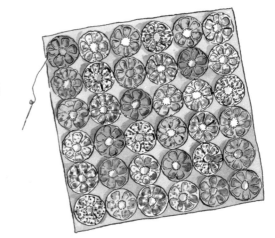

4 Lay the panel on the front of the cover and hand sew it in place by making a few stitches at the widest point of each rosette and a few stitches around the inner edges to hold everything securely in place.

As this is a hand-sewing project, it's a good way to introduce children to sewing. Do the cutting out and the pressing under of edges for them, and let them hand sew around the circles and gather them up to make the yo-yos. The pillow can be given a completely different look depending on what colors are chosen, and children will enjoy laying them out in different combinations.

tasseled pillow with silk panel

A strip of solid-colored silk, trimmed with bands of ribbon, forms the center panel of this pillow, contrasting beautifully with the elaborate fleur-de-lis fabric on either side. The center panel is small, so it's a great place to make the most of a piece of exquisite silk or embroidered upholstery fabric.

You will need

+ ½ yd. (40cm) of home decorating fabric, 54 in. (136cm) wide

+ 5¼ x 13¼ in. (14 x 33cm) rectangle of silk or embroidered upholstery fabric for the center panel

+ ¾ yd. (70cm) of ribbon or braid, 1 in. (2.5cm) wide

+ 10 in. (25cm) zipper

+ four tassels

+ 12 x 16 in. (30 x 40cm) pillow

+ matching sewing thread

1 Cut two 13¼ x 7¼ in. (33 x 17.5cm) rectangles of home decorating fabric for the front and two 17¼ x 7¼ in. (43 x 18cm) rectangles of the same fabric for the back. With right sides together, pin the two back pieces together along one long edge and mark 3⅝ in. (9cm) in from each end with pins. Machine stitch a ⅝ in. (1.5cm) seam up to the pins from each end. Now machine baste the center 10 in. (25cm). Press the seam open.

2 Pin the zipper into the basted part of the seam and hand baste it in place. Using a zipper foot on the machine, stitch the zipper in place from the right side. Remove the hand and machine basting. Open the zipper.

3 With right sides together, pin one front piece to the silk center panel along the long edges. machine stitch a ⅝ in. (1.5cm) seam. Pin and stitch the other front piece to the opposite side of the center panel in the same way. Press the seams open. Pin ribbon to each side of the center panel to cover the seam lines. Topstitch along both edges of each ribbon.

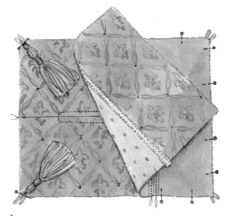

4 Pin one tassel at each corner on the right side of the pillow back, with the cords running out of the seam allowance and the tassels facing inward. With right sides together, pin the pillow front and back together so that the tassels are sandwiched in between. Machine stitch a ⅝ in. (1.5cm) seam around all four edges. Zigzag the raw edges. Turn the pillow cover right side out and press. Insert the pillow and close the zipper.

Silk fabrics lend themselves well to this idea, and a rectangular pillow made from three strips of silk always looks sumptuous. This is the time to indulge yourself by using a special fabric in the center panel which can be flanked by one or two solid colors. If you have found a small piece of embroidered silk at an antiques fair, or you have a fragment in a drawer that you've never known what to do with, this is your chance to bring it out and give it the attention it deserves.

eyelet-trimmed pillowcase

Cotton lace gives a vintage look to a crisp white pillowcase. A wide eyelet (broderie anglaise) border with a coordinating narrower insert makes the deep cuffs that overhang the side of the pillow. If you prefer, you could replace the cotton lace with strips cut from an openwork or embroidered fabric and simply seam them together.

You will need

+ 43 in. (110cm) length of cotton lace, 2 in. (5cm) wide

+ 43 in. (110cm) length of cotton lace, 8 in. (20cm) wide

+ ¾ yd. (70cm) white cotton sheeting

+ matching sewing thread

+ embroidery scissors or curved nail scissors

+ 20 × 30 in. (50 × 75cm) pillow

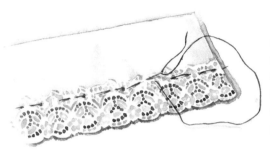

1 From the sheeting, cut out one 43 x 23 in. (110 x 58cm) rectangle and one 43 x 2½ in. (110 x 6cm) strip. Pin the narrow lace along the long edge of the strip of sheeting on the right side, overlapping the sheeting by ¾ in. (2cm). Baste securely in place, using small stitches so that it will not slip when machine stitched down.

2 Set the sewing machine to a ⅛ in. (3mm) closely spaced zigzag and fit the satin stitch foot, if you have one. Machine stitch over the edge of the lace, following the outline as closely as possible.

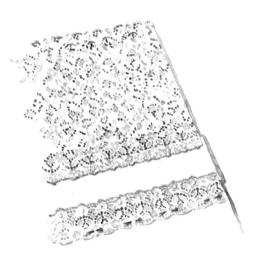

3 Attach the wide lace to the right side of the other long edge of the sheeting strip following the same method. Sew the other side of the narrow lace to one long edge of the rectangle of cotton sheeting in the same way.

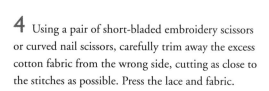

4 Using a pair of short-bladed embroidery scissors or curved nail scissors, carefully trim away the excess cotton fabric from the wrong side, cutting as close to the stitches as possible. Press the lace and fabric.

5 With right sides together, fold the pillowcase in half so that the lace forms a cuff, then pin and baste the raw edges together. Machine stitch a ½ in. (1cm) seam. Trim the seam allowance to ¼ in. (5mm) and finish the raw edges with a wide zigzag or overlock stitch. Turn the pillowcase right side out and press.

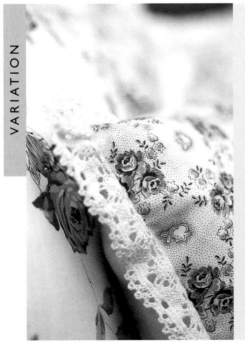

Find strips of old lace at antiques markets, or new pieces in your local notions (haberdashery) department, and then use them to trim readymade pillow covers or pillowcases. It's an instant way to add an antique look if you are decorating with vintage style in mind. Simply cut the strips of lace to the right length, turn under the raw ends, and slip stitch them in place.

embroidered pillowcase

The inspiration for the leaf pattern that decorates this pillowcase comes from the stylized embroidery of the 1950s, when designers looked to natural forms for inspiration. The stitches used are basic and the motifs can be worked quickly, but, if you prefer a more minimal look, work a single leaf in one corner or omit the embroidery altogether.

You will need

+ white cotton sheeting
+ tracing paper
+ 27 in. (68cm) square of cotton chambray
+ matching sewing thread
+ dressmaker's carbon paper
+ three 22 yd. (20m) skeins of thick (40) white coton à broder/mercerized thread
+ embroidery needle
+ 26 in. (66cm) square pillow

1 From cotton sheeting, cut out four 4 x 33 in. (10 x 84cm) border strips, one 10 x 33 in. (25 x 84cm) back piece, and one 26 x 33 in. (65 x 84cm) back piece. Cut an 8 x 27 in. (20 x 68cm) strip of tracing paper and fold in half lengthwise and crosswise. Line up the creases with the broken lines across the motif (see page 171) and trace the outline in pencil. Turn the paper over and trace a reversed motif above and below the first, using the part motifs as a placement guide. Mark the center of each edge of the chambray square. Matching the center of the paper to this point, pin the left edge to one edge of the fabric. Trace the design on to the right side of the fabric using dressmaker's carbon. Do the same on the other three edges.

2 Embroider the motif using coton à broder/mercerized thread. Use chain stitch for the leaf and top two spirals, three cross stitches for the leaf veins, stem stitch for the stalk and lower spirals, and detached chain stitch for the three lines of dots. Fill in the stalk with satin stitch. Press from the wrong side when complete.

3 Press both corners of each border strip inward at 90 degrees and trim off the excess fabric, leaving a ½ in. (1cm) seam allowance.

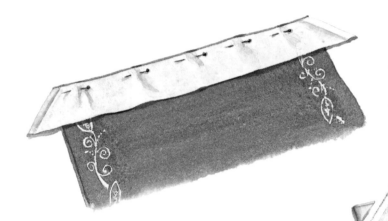

4 Pin and baste the shorter edge of one border strip centrally along one edge of the embroidered square. Machine stitch a ½ in. (1cm) seam between the crease lines, then press the seam outward.

5 Join the next strip to one adjacent side in the same way.

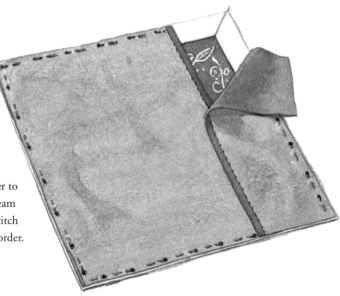

6 Line up the two diagonal sides of the strips and pin, then baste them together along the crease lines. Machine stitch together from the outside corner inward. Press the seam open, then add on the other two strips in the same way to complete the border.

7 Make a narrow double hem along one long side of each of the two back pieces. With right sides together and raw edges even, pin the wide piece of cotton sheeting along one edge of the chambray and the narrow piece along the opposite edge. Pin and machine stitch the front and back together with a ½ in. (1cm) seam. Trim the corners, turn right side out, and press. Baste the inside edge of the border to the back of the pillowcase just outside the seam line, making sure that it lies flat. Machine stitch ⅛ in. (3mm) inside the seam to make the border.

If you draw the line at embroidering your own fabric, why not commandeer a readymade throw or shawl to make two pillowcases? Use the tasseled and fringed edges on the right-hand end of one pillow and on the left-hand end of the other, and then use a plain edge on the ends that will meet in the middle of the bed.

Chair seat
cushions

Making seat pads can be as basic as a plain cushion to soften a garden chair or as involved as a mattress cushion for a kitchen bench seat, but they will all serve to make a hard wooden surface more comfortable. Most chair seat pads are held in place with ties made from the same fabric, so whether they are tailored and neatly fitting for a dining room, or squashy with ruffles for a breakfast room, they stay firmly in place.

mattress cushion

These chunky cushions, like scaled-down versions of a traditional mattress, make for comfortable seating and are a less formal alternative to tailored box cushions. A specially cut foam shape (which can be ordered from good upholstery stores or specialist retailers) is simply covered with functional cotton gingham or ticking and pulled together with big stitches to create the padded look.

You will need

+ thick cotton fabric
+ 4 x 16 x 16 in. (10 x 41 x 41cm) fire-retardant foam block
+ dressmaker's fading pen or tailor's chalk
+ long, straight upholsterer's needle
+ thick cotton yarn
+ ten 1 in. (2.5cm) self-cover buttons (optional)
+ matching sewing thread

1 From the cotton fabric, cut out a 3½ x 12 in. (9 x 30cm) strip for the handle, four 5 x 17 in. (13 x 43cm) boxing strips, and two 17 in. (43cm) squares for the top and bottom. Press under a ½ in. (1cm) seam allowances along all four edges of the handle strip, then press it in half lengthwise with wrong sides together. Baste the three open sides together and machine stitch ⅛ in. (3mm) from all four edges. Pin and baste the handle in place along the center of one of the boxing strips, looping it so that each end lies 4 in. (10cm) in from the short edge. Machine stitch several times across both ends of the handle.

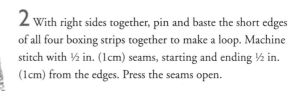

2 With right sides together, pin and baste the short edges of all four boxing strips together to make a loop. Machine stitch with ½ in. (1cm) seams, starting and ending ½ in. (1cm) from the edges. Press the seams open.

3 With right sides together and raw edges even, pin and baste one of the square panels to the side strips, matching the seams to the corners and allowing the seam allowances to open up at the corners. Stitch a ½ in. (1cm) seam. Make an extra line of stitching to reinforce each corner.

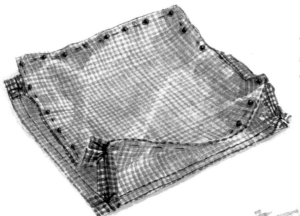

4 Turn the cover the other way up and, leaving the side opposite the handle unstitched, attach three edges of the second panel in the same way.

5 Press the seams open, then press under the seam allowances along the opening. Trim the corners and turn the cover right side out. Insert the foam block and slip stitch the opening closed.

6 Using a fading pen or tailor's chalk, mark a row of seven dots 2 in. (5cm) apart along each long edge of the cushion. Start 2 in. (5cm) from the corner and position them 1 in. (2.5cm) from the edge.

7 Thread an upholsterer's needle with a double length of yarn. Leaving a long tail, insert the point at the first mark along the top and bring the needle out through the foam at the first mark on the side. Reinsert the needle ¼ in. (5mm) to the right and bring it through again at the top ¼ in. (5mm) from the starting point. Knot the two ends of the yarn tightly and trim. Repeat all around the cushion, using the dots as a guide. Mark four points on the top and bottom of the cushion, each 5 in. (13cm) from the corner and make four more knots as before. For a larger cushion, cover ten self-cover buttons with fabric scraps and sew five to the top of the cushion and five to the back (one centrally and one in each corner).

Mattress cushions are an informal way to soften a chair seat, whether it's indoors or out. There's a softening of boundaries between indoors and out in contemporary design, and a set of aluminum garden chairs can be brought inside and used as dining seating, but they will need a bit of padding to make them comfortable. Combine a white-painted vintage table and bench with aluminum chairs and bring the look together with mattress cushions made from a faded, vintage-style fabric.

dining chair cushion

This pretty chair cushion is made from nine patchwork blocks of fabric, in which alternate blocks are made up of four small squares. Hand quilting has a charming quality and adds extra embellishment when done with colored embroidery thread. A ruffle finishes the cushion off beautifully, with the edges left unhemmed as a decorative detail.

You will need

+ 12 in. (30cm) square of each of two striped fabrics for the small patches

+ 25 x 5 in. (60 x 15cm) strip of floral fabric for the large patches

+ two 3½ x 46 in. (9 x 115cm) strips of striped fabric for the ruffle

+ two 2 x 25 in. (5 x 64cm) strips of striped fabric for the ties

+ 13 in. (32cm) square of striped fabric for the back

+ 13 in. (32cm) square of batting (wadding)

+ embroidery floss and needle

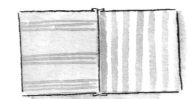

1 Measure and cut eight 3 in. (7cm) squares of each of the two striped fabrics. With right sides together, pin and stitch one square of each together with a ½ in. (1cm) seam, and press the seam open. Repeat for the remaining seven pairs.

2 With right sides together, join two pairs of the squares from step 1 with a ½ in. (1cm) seam; press open. Repeat to make four patchwork squares.

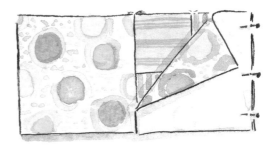

3 Using the floral fabric, measure and cut five 5 in. (12cm) squares. With right sides together, join one of these to one of the patchwork squares with a ½ in. (1cm). Stitch another flower fabric square to the other side of the patchwork square and press the seams open.

4 Make the central strip by joining two patchwork squares to either side of a floral fabric square in the same way as in step 3 and make the bottom strip as for the top strip. Join these three strips with a ½ in. (1cm) seam, forming a 13 in. (32cm) square with alternating floral and patchwork squares. Press the seams open.

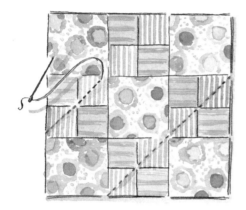

5 Cut a piece of batting (wadding) 13 in. (32cm) square and pin the patchwork, right side up, onto it. Using the embroidery floss, sew neat running stitches diagonally across the striped fabric squares in both directions.

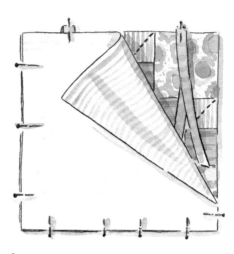

6 Make the ties by folding the two strips in half lengthwise, and folding each long edge into the middle. Press and stitch. Fold these in half and place on the patchwork panel as shown. Lay the back on top of the patchwork with right sides together and raw edges even. Pin and stitch the layers together with a ½ in. (1cm) seam, leaving an opening of about 6 in. (15cm) along one edge. Trim the corners and turn right side out. Slip stitch the opening closed. Press the cushion.

7 With right sides together, join the two ruffle strips at the ends with a ½ in. (1cm) seam to form a strip 80 in. (200cm) long. Machine stitch along one long edge to prevent raveling. Sew running stitches along the other edge of the strip and pull the thread to gather it so that it fits around three sides of the cushion. Sew a few stitches in the end to hold in place.

8 Hand sew or machine stitch the ruffle around the cushion on the right side, turning under the ends and hand sewing them in place. Press carefully.

A slightly more structured ruffle-edged cushion is ideal for a country
kitchen, especially when placed on a wooden chair that has been painted
in a contrasting color. Make a ruffled cushion as for the Double-Ruffle
Taffeta pillow (see pages 44–46), but make only one ruffle strip and attach
it to three sides instead of four. Make and attach four ties for the back
edge, as in step 6 of the Dining Chair Cushion.

child's seat cushion

Making a cushion for a simple wooden chair can add a lovely decorative touch. This patchwork star is a slightly more complex design, but can easily be made using a sewing machine. It can be made to fit any size of seat by increasing the sizes of the patterns accordingly. A cute pompom fringe finishes the cushion off beautifully, and fabric ties are added to hold it in place.

You will need

+ 14 × 18 in. (35 × 45cm) of each of two fabrics, for the star

+ 18 in. (45cm) square of fabric, for the back and ties

+ 20 × 16 in. (50 × 40cm) piece (approx) of polkadot fabric, for the small triangles

+ 16 in. (40cm) square (approx) of checked fabric, for the large triangles

+ 12 in. (30cm) square of washable heavyweight batting (wadding)

+ 1 ⅜ yd. (1.2m) of pompom fringe

+ paper for pattern

+ matching sewing thread

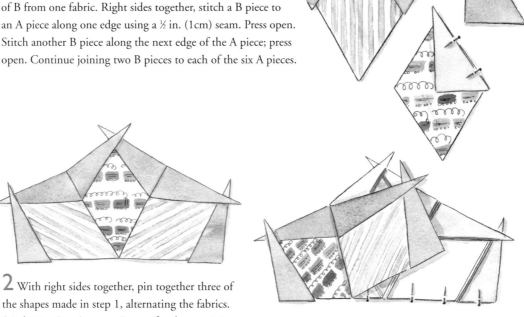

1 Using the templates on page 172, cut out patterns A (diamond), B (small triangle), and C (large triangle). Cut out three pieces of A from each of two fabrics, and 12 pieces of B from one fabric. Right sides together, stitch a B piece to an A piece along one edge using a ½ in. (1cm) seam. Press open. Stitch another B piece along the next edge of the A piece; press open. Continue joining two B pieces to each of the six A pieces.

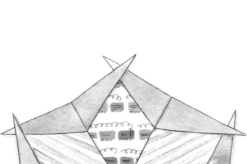

2 With right sides together, pin together three of the shapes made in step 1, alternating the fabrics. Stitch ½ in. (1cm) seams. Repeat for the remaining three shapes. Press all the seams open.

3 Again with right sides together, pin and stitch these two half-hexagons together with a ½ in. (1cm) seam, and press the seam open. Trim off any bits of seam allowance that stick out beyond the edge.

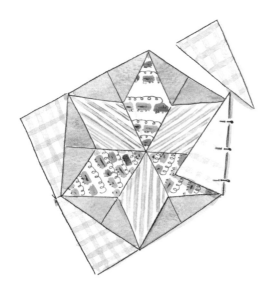

4 Lay the patchwork star on the work surface with one of its points at the top. Using pattern piece C, cut four large triangles from the checked fabric. With right sides together, pin them to the four corners of the hexagon. Press the seams open.

5 Measure and cut two 1½ × 18 in. (4 × 45cm) strips of the fabric for the back and ties. Fold both strips in half lengthwise and press. Fold the edges into the center fold and press. Pin and stitch along the length of both.

6 Cut the back piece to the same size as the patchwork panel.
Pin and baste the bobble fringe all the way around the right
side of the patchwork panel, with the pompoms pointing
inward. Fold the ties in half and position them at the top
of the patchwork panel 1 in. (3cm) from the top
corners. Place the back and the patchwork
panel with right sides together and pin.
Stitch a ½ in. (1cm) seam all the
way around, leaving an
opening of about 4 in.
(10cm) along the top
edge. Turn right side
out. Cut a piece of batting
(wadding) to fit the cover and
push into the cover. Hand sew
the opening closed. Press.

A pompom trim is a classic addition to any
cushion, whether patchwork or animal print. You
can buy the trim with different-sized pompoms
and in many colors. Some trims are inserted into
the seam, as in the Child's Seat Cushion,
while others are sewn on top, as here.

chair back cover and cushion

If you find your home is filled with flea-market treasures, here's a simple idea for bringing a collection of chairs together with a uniform look. This pretty set, consisting of back cover and cushion, is easier to make than fitted slipcovers, and the dimensions can easily be adjusted to suit different chair sizes. A simple fabric "envelope" covers the chair back, while a seat cushion covered in the same fabric neatens the whole scheme.

You will need

+ printed cotton fabric
+ square cushion
+ thick piping cord, enough to go around the edge of the pillow
+ 1¼ yd. (1.15m) of white cotton tape, ⅜ in. (1cm) wide
+ matching sewing thread
+ two ⅝ in. (15mm) buttons
+ dressmaker's fading pen or tailor's chalk

TIP

For extra comfort, if you wish, you could also add a layer of batting (wadding) to the back cover, to soften the back of the chair.

1 Measure the size of your cushion. Cut out two square pieces from fabric to these measurements, adding a ⅝ in. (1.5cm) seam allowance all around. Cut out a smaller rectangular piece the size of the cushion, by two-thirds the width, adding a ⅝ in. (1.5cm) seam allowance all around.

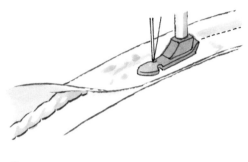

2 Measure around the circumference of your piping cord and cut out a bias-grain fabric strip to this measurement (see page 169), by the required length, adding a ⅝ in. (1.5cm) seam allowance to all sides. To cover the cord, place the piping cord down the center of the bias strip on the wrong side. Bring the long edges together around the cord and stitch down the length close to the cord, using a zipper foot or piping cord on your machine.

3 Place the piping on the right side of one of the fabric squares, with cord facing inward and raw edges even. To help the piping go around the corners, snip into the seam allowances to help it bend. Baste the piping in place.

4 To join the ends of the piping cord, unpick the machine stitches for about 2 in. (5cm) at each end and fold back the bias strip. Trim the two cord ends so they butt together, then bind the ends together with thread. Turn under ¼ in. (5mm) of fabric at one end of the bias strip, and slip this end over the raw opposite end. Baste ends neatly in place.

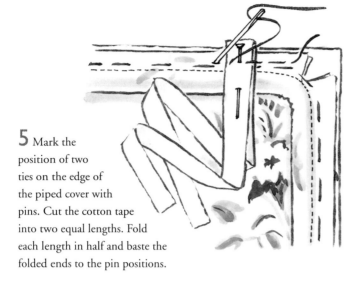

5 Mark the position of two ties on the edge of the piped cover with pins. Cut the cotton tape into two equal lengths. Fold each length in half and baste the folded ends to the pin positions.

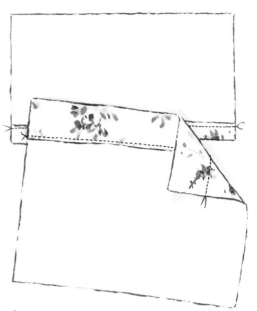

6 On the remaining fabric square, press under a double-turned 1¾ in. (4.5cm) hem along one edge and stitch in place. On the rectangular piece, press under a double-turned ¾ in. (2cm) hem down one long edge and stitch in place.

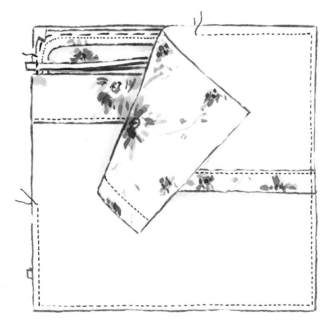

7 Lay the piped cover right side up on a flat surface and place the larger hemmed piece right side down on top, with raw edges even. Place the rectangular piece on top, overlapping the hemmed edges and keeping raw edges even. Pin, baste, and machine stitch the layers together close to the cord, using a zipper foot or piping foot on your machine and sandwiching the ties in place at the same time. Turn the cover right side out and press. Make buttonholes on the overlap of the back opening. Sew buttons to the underlap of the back in line with the buttonholes.

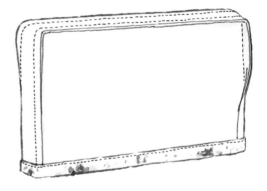

8 Measure the width and depth of your chair back. Cut two pieces of fabric to these measurements, adding a ⅝ in. (1.5cm) seam all around. Cut a boxing strip 2 in. (5cm) wide by the width of the chair back plus twice the depth, adding 1¼ in. (3cm) to the length for seams. With right sides together, stitch the strip between the two fabric pieces. Turn the cover right side out and press. Press a ¼ in. (5mm) hem to the wrong side along the lower edge, then a further ⅜ in. (1cm). Machine stitch in place.

Furnishing your home with flea-market finds is an excellent way to add style on a budget, and wooden chairs can be painted to be used in any room in the house. To make them more comfortable and to inject pattern and color, tie on simple knife-edge cushions. Having no boxing strip, they are faster to make than traditional box cushions, and for an ultra-quick version you could omit piping, too. Whether they are made from vintage flour-sack linen or a traditional-looking print, a cushion with added ties will be both decorative and practical.

garden chair set

Paired with a small back cover, this ruffled seat cushion adds a touch of comfort to a simple garden chair and brings a delightfully summery feel to any patio or garden. Here a vintage-style floral fabric is used, trimmed with a dainty ruffle made from a coordinating polkadot fabric. The matching cover, which could easily be padded for more comfort, sits snugly on the chair back.

You will need

+ ¾ yd. (70cm) floral fabric, 45 in. (115cm) wide
+ ¼ yd. (20cm) polkadot fabric, 45 in. (115cm) wide
+ 10 in. (25cm) zipper
+ matching sewing thread
+ foam pad to fit chair

1 Make a paper pattern of your chair seat, adding ½ in. (1.5cm) all around for the seam allowances. Fold the floral fabric in half to form two layers, and pin the paper pattern to it. Pin the pattern in place and cut out the fabric.

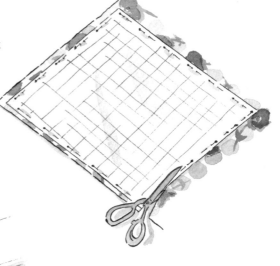

2 For the ruffle, cut a 4 x 78in. (10 x 200cm) length of polkadot fabric. (Join pieces together as necessary to make the required length and press open the seams.) Press under ⅜ in. (1cm) and then ½ in. (1.5cm) along one long edge and both ends. Pin and machine stitch.

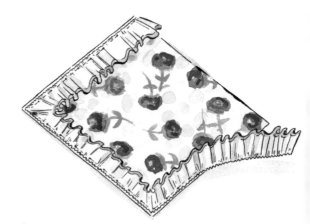

3 Sew a loose running stitch along the length of the strip, about ⅜ in. (1cm) from the raw edge. Gently pull the thread to gather the fabric, making sure that the gathers are even. The finished ruffle should be the same length as the side and front edges of the seat. Finish with a few small stitches.

4 Lay one of the floral pieces right side up on your work surface. With right sides together, aligning the raw edges, pin the ruffle around the sides and front edge, and baste in place.

5 To make the ties, cut four 2¼ x 17¼ in. (6 x 45cm) strips of floral fabric. Press under. Press under ½ in. (1.5cm) on one end and both long sides. Fold the strip in half lengthwise, aligning the edges. Pin and machine stitch along the turned-under end and along the length, stitching as close to the edge as possible. Repeat with the other three pieces of fabric.

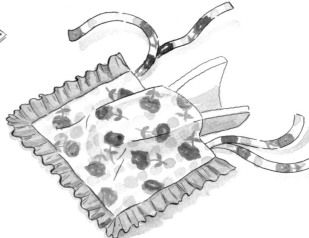

6 Lay the cushion piece with the ruffle right side up on your work surface. Aligning the raw edges, pin and baste two pairs of ties along the back edge of the cushion piece, placing each pair about 2 in. (5cm) from one side edge (depending upon the design of your chair).

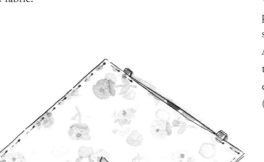

7 With right sides together, pin the two cushion pieces together along the back edge, sandwiching the ruffle in between. Machine stitch a ½ in. (1.5cm) seam along the back edge, leaving a 10 in. (25cm) opening. Baste the opening and press open the seam. Pin and baste the zipper into the basted part of the seam. Machine stitch in place from the right side, using a zipper foot on your machine. Remove the basting. Open the zipper.

8 Pin and stitch the three other sides of the cushion cover. Make small snips at the corners. Turn the cover right side out and press. Insert the cushion pad and close the zipper.

9 To make the back cover, measure and cut two rectangles of floral fabric 9 in. (23cm) deep, and as wide as the chair back plus 2½ in. (4cm) for seam allowances and ease. With right sides together, pin and stitch the fabric pieces together along three sides with a ½ in. (1.5cm) seam. Trim the corners. On the remaining raw edge, press under a double ⅜ in. (1cm) hem. Pin and machine stitch in place. Turn the cover right side out and press.

Old wood-slatted garden chairs are perfect for the conservatory or out under the trees, but they can be uncomfortable if you sit on them for too long. Line the fabric of the cushion and the back cover with a sheet of thin foam and the chair will be transformed.

kitchen chair cushion

Wooden kitchen chairs are practical, but they do need padding to make them comfortable. A tailored knife-edge cushion is a smart way to soften the seat and bring style to the kitchen—and by cutting the foam pillow pad to the exact shape of the chair seat, you can get a really precise fit. Blue and white gingham will brighten up even the most jaded kitchen decor, and the sprigs of yellow flowers on this fabric add a hint of early-morning summer sunshine.

You will need

+ pattern paper
+ foam 1 in. (2.5 cm) thick
+ home decorating fabric for the top and back
+ 12 × 20 in. (30 × 50cm) piece of coordinating fabric for the ties
+ fabric cut on the bias and about 2 yd. (2m) of piping cord, or 2 yd. (2m) of readymade piping
+ 10 in. (25cm) zipper
+ matching sewing thread

1 Fold the pattern paper in half and place it on the chair seat, aligning the midpoint of the chair with the fold of the paper. Draw around the edge of the seat. Draw a second line ⅝ in. (1.5cm) outside the first, for the seam allowance. Cut out the pattern and open out the pattern paper. Cut one piece of fabric for the top and one for the back. Using a sharp craft knife, cut the foam to the same size as the pattern minus the seam allowance.

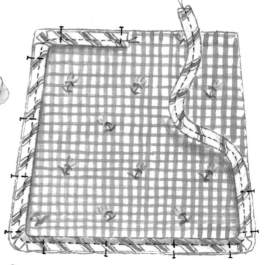

2 Make a strip of piping long enough to fit around the cushion. Pin and baste it around the right side of the top, with the raw edge facing outward and the piped edge just inside the seamline. which is ⅝ in. (1.5cm) from the edge. Snip into the piping seam allowance at the corners. Join the ends of the cord.

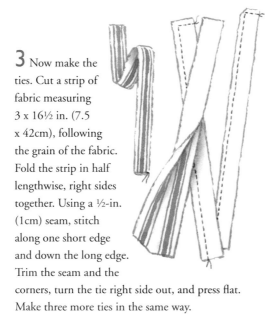

3 Now make the ties. Cut a strip of fabric measuring 3 × 16½ in. (7.5 × 42cm), following the grain of the fabric. Fold the strip in half lengthwise, right sides together. Using a ½-in. (1cm) seam, stitch along one short edge and down the long edge. Trim the seam and the corners, turn the tie right side out, and press flat. Make three more ties in the same way.

4 With raw edges even, pin and baste two ties to the right side of the back edge of the cushion back, approximately 2 in. (5cm) in from each side edge, depending on the design of your chair.

Another way of securing a cushion pad to a chair is to attach two long ties to each corner, and tie them in a bow around each leg.

5 Right sides together, pin the pillow back to the top along the back edge. Machine stitch a ⅝ in. (1.5cm) seam, leaving a 10 in. (25cm) opening in the center. Machine baste the opening. Press open the seam. Pin and hand baste the closed zipper, face down, into the basted part of the seam. Put the zipper foot on the machine and stitch the zipper in place from the right side. Remove the hand and machine basting. Open the zipper.

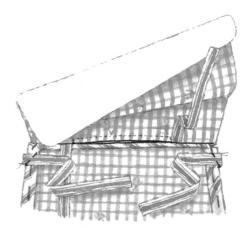

6 On the right side of the cushion back, pin and baste the remaining two ties to the side edges of the pillow back, 1 in. (2.5cm) down from the back edge. Right sides together, pin the top of the pillow to the back along the side and front edges. Stitch close to the stitching line of the piping. Turn the cover right side out and press. Insert the foam pad and close the zipper.

Equipment, techniques, & templates

sewing equipment
Get together a well-stocked sewing box before you start, and you'll be ready to tackle any of the projects in this book.

Sewing kit

For the projects in this book you will need just a few basic tools. Good scissors are essential, including a pair of large, cutting-out shears, medium-size dressmaker's scissors, and small embroidery scissors for snipping threads. Pinking shears are useful for finishing raw edges and making decorative edgings.

Use good-quality steel dressmaking pins which will not rust or go blunt: keep them in a box so they stay sharp. Choose your needle according to the weight of the fabric and the thickness of the thread, and use a special needle for embroidery.

An iron is invaluable for pressing seams, but it should be used with a damp cloth to protect delicate fabrics. Other useful items to have on hand are a seam ripper to unpick seams, a blunt pencil or knitting needle for pushing out corners, and a thimble.

Measuring and marking tools

Use a long, straight ruler along with a tape measure, and double check all measurements. Remember only to follow one set of the measurements given in the projects (either standard or metric), as they are not interchangeable. For drawing circles, use a compass. For specific designs that need to be scaled up and down, use graph paper, and you can purchase special paper for cutting out patterns.

When marking up fabric, tailor's chalk is easy to apply and remove and comes in a variety of colors to suit your fabric; or you could use a dressmaker's fading pen (testing it first on a scrap of fabric to make sure it leaves absolutely no mark on the right side of the fabric). Alternatively, use contrasting basting thread to make several small, loose loops that can be snipped away without trace.

Fabrics

Choose the type of fabric according to the function of the pillow. Home decorating fabrics are best for most pillows; use tougher cloth for floor pillows, outdoor pillows, and cushions; and delicate fabrics for more decorative pillows.

Check how much a fabric is likely to shrink when laundered because you may need to buy up to a third more material to compensate for this; if possible pick a colorfast cloth. If the fabric is machine-washable, it's advisable to machine wash in order it to preshrink it before cutting, in case different sections shrink at different rates.

If you are using fabric that is not quite large enough, you can join sections of fabric on borders and back panels of pillows, provided you carefully match the pattern.

Pads and fillings

Pillows to use inside the covers you make come in a variety of shapes and sizes and with different fillings. The most luxurious filling is feather and down, which should be used sparingly in a puffy scatter pillow or more densely to stuff a firm seat cover.

If you make your own pillow with a feather filling, use a downproof fabric such as a thick, close-weave cotton, otherwise sharp feather ends will protrude. Plain cotton or muslin fabric is suitable for use with polyester fiberfill stuffing.

Do not allow feather or synthetic pillows to get wet, as they are very absorbent. Plastic or latex foam chips are lumpy and uncomfortable but nonabsorbent so they are useful for outdoor furnishings.

Foam blocks can be cut to size and are used to form cushions for seating. Cover the blocks with batting (wadding) first to smooth out the corners.

sewing techniques

The techniques in the projects involve both hand and machine stitches; the more complicated ones are outlined below. If desired, all the pillows can be completed by using a hand backstitch instead of the machine stitch indicated in the instructions. Make sure you work in either standard or metric measurements, not a combination.

Running or gathering stitch

A series of small, neat stitches, equal in length on both sides of the fabric. Running stitch is used to gather cloth by hand. Knot the thread at one end and sew two parallel rows of running stitches close together along the length to be gathered. Wind the loose threads at the other end around a pin and pull gently to form even gathers.

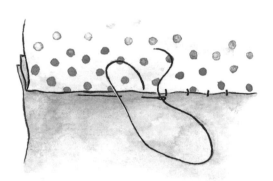

Slip stitch

A simple way to join two folded edges. Knot the end of the thread and working from right to left, insert the needle and slip it through the fold for about ¼ in. (5mm). On the other piece of fabric, pick up a couple of threads to join the two edges. The stitches should be almost invisible, so keep them small. Slip stitch is easy to unpick if, say, you want to remove a pillow cover for washing.

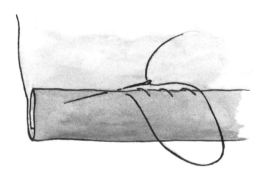

Hemming stitch

Use this stitch to hold a folded edge to flat fabric. Sewing a hem by hand produces a much neater result than machine hemming. On the wrong side catch a couple of threads from the flat fabric; with the needle pointing diagonally from right to left, slide it under the folded edge and bring it up through both layers of the fold. Most hems are turned under twice, but for heavy fabrics make a single turn, after finishing the exposed raw edge (see page 167).

Back stitch

This is used for creating a sturdy seam that can be used as an alternative to machine stitching, or for finishing thread ends securely by sewing a few stitches on top of one another as an alternative to making a knot, or for embroidery. After completing a stitch, insert the needle at the end of the previous stitch; bring it out a stitch length in front of the thread to create a solid line of stitching on the right side and an overlapping effect on the underside.

Cross stitch

This embroidery stitch can be worked as single stitches or multiple stitches, either horizontally, vertically, or diagonally. When working in a line, stitch half of each cross (all slanting the same way) before returning back along the line to complete the other half of each cross.

Feather stitch

Work this decorative stitch on the right side of the fabric. Bring the needle through at A, insert at B, bring through again at C, looping the thread under the needle before pulling it through. Repeat the process by inserting the needle at D, coming out at E and looping the thread under the needle once again. Repeat this pattern, alternating the looped stitches on either side of the central line.

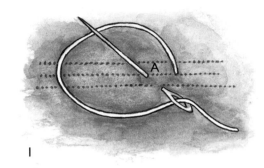

1

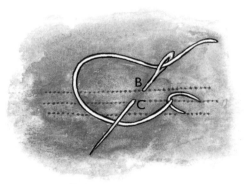

2

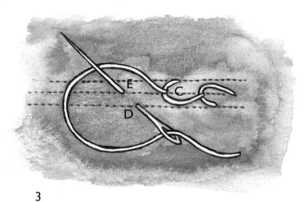

3

Blanket stitch

A decorative stitch for finishing edges. Secure the thread at one end of the fabric, and working from right to left, insert the needle about ½ in. (1 cm) from the edge; keeping the thread under the point of the needle, complete the stitch to create a loop. Continue to work the stitches every ½ in. (1cm) or so, making sure the height is even.

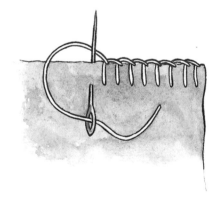

Buttonhole stitch

Although buttonholes can be made on the sewing machine, they can also be made by hand using this stitch. It is both decorative and strengthening as it prevents fraying of the cut edges to accommodate the button.

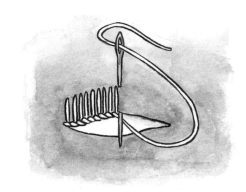

Work on the right side of the fabric using a short needle and a strong thread with a knotted end. Hide the knot on the wrong side of the fabric and work with the cut edge on the right (or on the left if you are left-handed).

Insert the needle at right angles to the cut edge, taking a stitch through the fabric; loop the thread behind the needle before pulling through to form a knot on the cut edge with each stitch. Keep the stitches evenly spaced, maintain an even tension on each knot, and aim for the knots to touch each other. Fan the stitches close together around both ends of the hole to prevent tearing. The more the fabric will ravel, the deeper your stitches should be.

Seams

Stitch seams from top to bottom, making sure that patterned fabrics run the same way on each side. The most commonly used seam is the flat seam; place the fabric right sides together with raw edges even and pin, baste, and machine stitch to join, making a few backstitches to secure the threads at the end.

For heavy fabrics trim the seam allowance close to the stitching to reduce bulk. If the seam is to be pressed to one side, use a grading technique by cutting only one seam allowance back to create a smoother surface on the right side of the material. If the cloth is likely to ravel, finish the raw edges (see right).

Finishing seams

There are three ways to finish seams to neaten and strengthen them. On fabric that is not liable to fray, you can either leave the seam allowance untrimmed, although you should finish the corners (see page 168), or else pink the raw edges with pinking shears.

To finish a seam by hand, use overcasting (oversewing), in which you hold the needle diagonally and take even stitches ⅛–¼ in. (3–5mm) apart. To finish a raw edge by machine, you can use a small and narrow zigzag, working the zigzagging over the raw edge, or overlock with a serger.

Finishing corners and curves

Although it is not strictly necessary to finish seams, as the allowances lie inside the pillow cover and are not visible, for good results you should pay some attention to corners and curves.

To create a neat pointed corner, stitch right up to the corner, leave the needle in the fabric, raise the machine foot and pivot the fabric through 90 degrees, then lower the foot and continue stitching. Trim the seam allowance across the corner so you can push the finished corner out to a neat point.

For sharp angles, work one or two stitches across the point to strengthen it.

When sewing a curved seam, keep a uniform seam allowance. For concave (inward-facing) curves, clip little notches to achieve a flat finish (see below left). For convex (outward-facing) curves, cut small slits into the seam allowance (see below right).

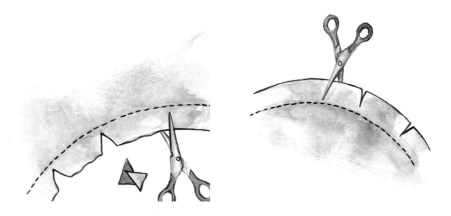

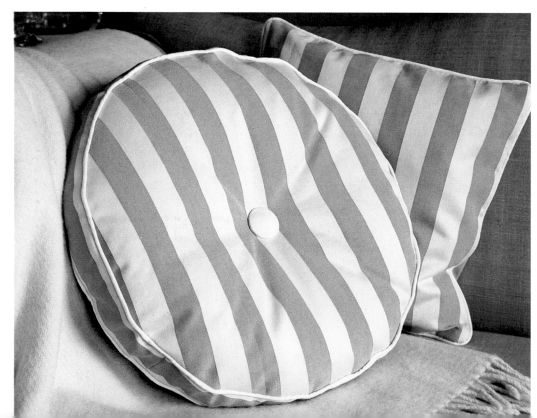

Bias binding and piping

Bias binding is the term given to strips of fabric cut on the diagonal grain; it is used to cover piping cord. Both bias binding and piping cord are available readymade, but you can create much more versatile matching or contrasting trimmings yourself by making up your own.

Choose a fabric of the same type and weight as the body of the pillow to avoid problems of shrinking and bunching after washing. Flat piping refers to a bias strip used folded in half without the cord inserted. Piping cord is available in different thickness, so choose an appropriate width. For safety, wash cotton cord to preshrink it before you begin sewing, or the piping may pucker later. Likewise, make sure that purchased piping and bias binding are shrinkproof and colorfast before sewing.

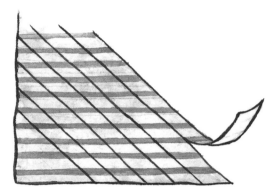 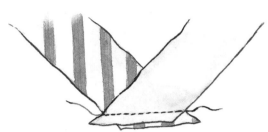

To make bias strips for bias binding, take a square of fabric and fold a straight raw edge parallel to the selvage (the non-fray woven edge) to form a triangle. The bottom of the triangle (opposite the right angle) is the bias line. Use a long ruler to mark a series of lines parallel to the bias line, according to the width you need (see above). The bias binding must be wide enough to cover the cord comfortably with an additional seam allowance of ½ in. (1cm) or ⅝ in. (1.5cm) —whatever seam allowance you are using for the project. Join enough strips (see right) to cover the cord for the length of piping you need.

Cut out and join bias strips right sides together along the short ends with a flat seam (see above). Press the seam and trim the corners to lie flat with the bias strip.

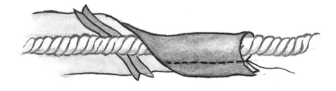

Wrap the binding, right side out, around the cord. Pin and baste, then machine stitch close to the cord (see above). Pin, baste, and stitch piping to the right side of one fabric piece, so the cord lies just inside the seam line and the raw edges are even with those of the fabric piece. Clip the seam allowance on the bias strip up to the stitching at corners. Where the ends of the piping meet, trim the cord so the ends butt together, and trim the binding so there is an overlap of ½ in. (1cm). Turn under ½ in. (1cm) at one end of the binding, and tuck the opposite raw edge inside. When the other fabric piece is stitched to the first, right sides together, the piping will be sandwiched between them.

Transferring a design

If your pattern is actual size, it can be traced directly onto tracing paper or transfer paper. If it has to be enlarged, transfer the pattern onto graph paper and increase the proportion to the desired size; or use a photocopier to enlarge it. After you have done this, rule horizontal and vertical lines through the center of the design.

Iron the piece of cloth you are going to embroider and fold it in half vertically. Open out the fold and sew a straight line of basting stitches down the middle. Repeat to divide and mark the cloth in half along the horizontal to give you a guide for plotting the pattern. Use transfer paper or dressmaker's carbon paper, which is non-smudge and comes in several colors (available from most fabric stores). Choose a paper that contrasts well with the fabric so the design shows up. Place the fabric right side up on a hard surface and place the transfer paper shiny side down over it. Place the tracing paper over the transfer paper and line up the horizontal and vertical lines, then pin all three layers together. Trace over the design with a ballpoint pen or a pencil. Carefully remove the tracing and transfer papers and begin to stitch, following the imprint of the design.

Work from the center outward, as marked previously. The cross stitches should extend slightly beyond the carbon paper lines so they are not visible on the finished fabric. Remove the basting stitches once the embroidery is complete.

For this design (featured in the Initials in Cross Stitch project on pages 116–118), it is necessary to double the size of the pattern before transferring it to the fabric; use one of the methods explained above. To add a personal touch to your pillow, insert the initials of your choice instead of using the ones given here. To do this, leave a gap where the A and B are and replace them with small crosses marking your new letters.

These leaf templates are used in the
Autumnal Appliqué project on pages
120–121. Enlarge by 200% or use at
whatever size you wish.

Use this design for the Embroidered
Pillowcase project on pages 138–140.
Either trace to use at this size, or enlarge
to fit your own pillowcase.

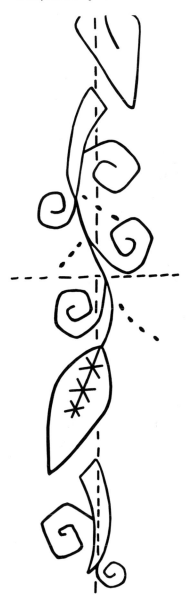

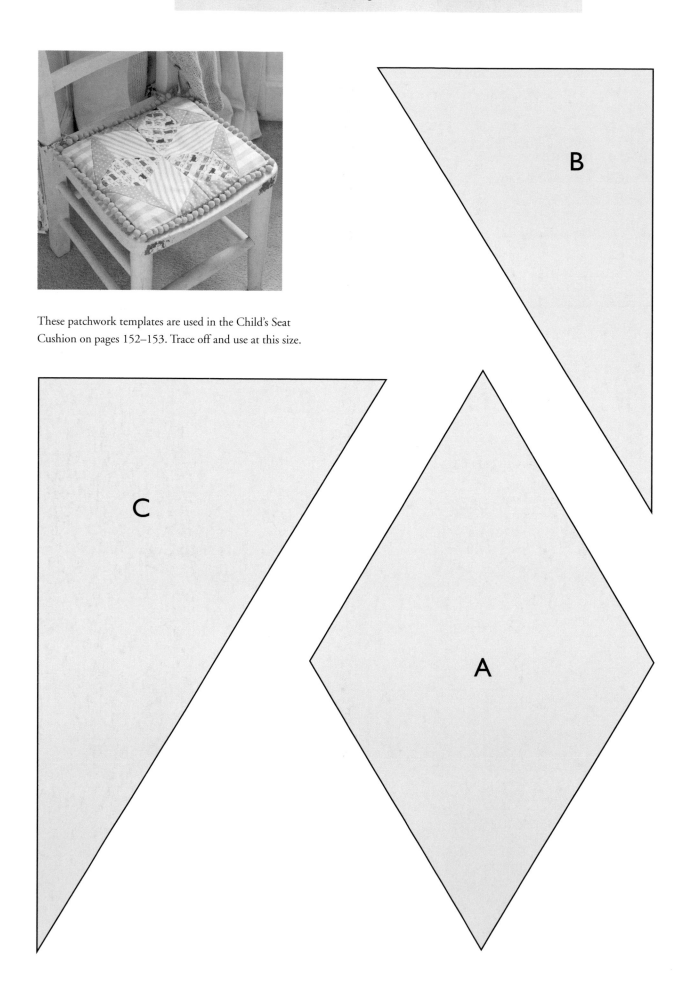

These patchwork templates are used in the Child's Seat
Cushion on pages 152–153. Trace off and use at this size.

These animal faces are used in the Pyramid Beanbag project on pages 110–111. Enlarge by 200% or use at whatever size you wish.

Key: a = above, b = below, c = center, l = left, r = right

Project-makers

Jane Bolsover: 76–78

Katrin Cargill: 22–23, 35, 42–43, 44–46, 48–49 (inspired by Wendy Harrop), 50–52, 62–64, 96–98, 116–118, 120–121, 160–170

Charlotte Casadejus: 21b

Lucinda Ganderton: 32–34, 86–87, 102–104, 110–111, 136–137, 138–140, 144–146

Lucinda Ganderton/Karen Nicol: 38–39

Lucinda Ganderton/Jane Sacchi: 12–14

Lucinda Ganderton/Karen Spurgin: 114–115

Pat Giddens: 15

Emma Hardy: 26–27, 28–30, 56–57, 70–72, 74–75, 84–85, 100–101, 106–108, 124–125, 126–127, 132–133, 148–150, 152–153, 158–160

Gloria Nicol: 36–37, 54–55, 58–59, 66–67, 68–69, 92–94, 134–135, 162–163

Hikaru Noguchi: 128–130

Flora Roberts: 80–83

Lucy Salem: 57b

Christina Strutt: 24–25, 90–91

Christina Strutt/Jane Bolsover: 16–19, 20–21, 122–123, 154–156

Catherine Woram: 131

Caroline Zoob: 87b

Illustration

Trina Dalziel: 76, 78

Michael A Hill: 26, 28, 30, 56–57, 70, 72, 74, 84, 100–101, 106, 108, 124–125, 126, 132, 148, 150, 152–153, 158, 160, 172

Jacqueline Pestell: 22–23, 42–43, 44, 46, 48–49, 50, 52, 62, 64, 96, 98, 116, 118, 120–121, 128, 130, 165–170, 171l

Lizzie Sanders: 12, 14, 32, 34, 38, 86–87, 102, 104, 110–111, 114–115, 136–137, 138, 140, 144, 146, 171r, 173

Kate Simunek: 16, 18–19, 20, 24, 36–37, 54–55, 58–59, 66, 68–69, 90, 92, 94, 122, 134, 154, 156, 162–163

Photography

Caroline Arber: 73, 87b

Simon Brown: 36b, 58, 77, 85b, 121b, 125b, 135b

Lisa Cohen: 23r (home of designer Clare Tweed, www.sashawaddell.com), 25b, 67b (home of designer Clare Tweed), 79 (Amsterdam apartment designed by Marijke van Nunen), 99 (styled by Kate French, cushions www. etoilehome.com), 105, 111r (www. tapet-cafe.dk), 115b (Amsterdam apartment designed by Marijke van Nunen), 127b, 147a&b (designer Nina Hartmann's Swedish home, www.vintagebynina.com), 163r

Vanessa Davies: 131

Christopher Drake: 83

Catherine Gratwicke: 57b, 122

Sandra Lane: 4a, 5a, 13 (home of Paul Balland and Jane Wadham, jwflowers.com), 14, 15, 21b, 31, 39a (home of Karen Nicol and Peter Clark, www.karennicol.com), 87a, 89l, 103, 111l, 113l, 115a (styled by Lucinda Ganderton), 133b, 137a (home of Patty Collister, An Angel At My Table), 137b, 139, 141, 143r, 145, 171r, 173

James Merrell: 2, 3, 5b, 8, 23l, 33 (styled by Kristin Perers), 40l&r, 41l, 43a, 45, 47, 48a&b, 49b, 51, 53, 55b, 60r, 63, 64, 69b, 89r, 95, 97, 112l&r, 117, 119, 121a, 129 (styled by Katrin Cargill), 153b, 170, 171l

Gloria Nicol: 5c, 7, 36a, 55a, 59, 60l, 61l, 67a, 69a, 81, 88r, 93, 135a, 142r, 163l, 168

Debbie Patterson: 4b, 6, 9, 11l, 27a, 28b, 29, 41r, 57a, 61r, 65, 71, 72, 74a, 85a, 101a, 107, 113r, 125a, 127a, 133a, 142l, 143l, 149, 153a, 159, 160, 172

Mark Scott: 27b, 39b, 43b, 74b, 101b, 109, 151, 161

Lucinda Symons: 1, 4c, 10r, 11r, 17, 21a, 91b, 123, 155, 157b

Polly Wreford/Sasha Waddell: 157a

Edina van der Wyck: 10l, 19, 25a, 88l, 91a